MIND BODY AWAKENING

Your Spiritual Tool Book

Ewa Demahina

BALBOA.PRESS

A DIVISION OF HAY HOUSE

Balboa Press books may be ordered through booksellers or by contacting:

Balboa Press
A Division of Hay House
1663 Liberty Drive
Bloomington, IN 47403
www.balboapress.com
1 (877) 407-4847

Because of the dynamic nature of the Internet, any web addresses or links contained in this book may have changed since publication and may no longer be valid. The views expressed in this work are solely those of the author and do not necessarily reflect the views of the publisher, and the publisher hereby disclaims any responsibility for them.

The author of this book does not dispense medical advice or prescribe the use of any technique as a form of treatment for physical, emotional, or medical problems without the advice of a physician, either directly or indirectly. The intent of the author is only to offer information of a general nature to help you in your quest for emotional and spiritual well-being. In the event you use any of the information in this book for yourself, which is your constitutional right, the author and the publisher assume no responsibility for your actions.

Any people depicted in stock imagery provided by Getty Images are models, and such images are being used for illustrative purposes only.
Certain stock imagery © Getty Images.

Print information available on the last page.

ISBN: 978-1-9822-4531-3 (sc)
ISBN: 978-1-9822-4536-8 (e)

Balboa Press rev. date: 06/19/2020

SOMETHING SACRED

For me Healing is sacred. A tool which I have calibrated my body, my mind, as well as my soul over many years and I never seem to get tired of exploring more and go deeper within myself with this tool. I will always remember my first encounter with healing. This first time it was a Reiki healing workshop that was on my agenda. I had absolutely no idea what the weekend would contain. For months this word Reiki surrounded me and in the end it was really in my face and I couldn't neglect the "universal signs" any more. I had made a decision that I would dedicate my time for a few months to attend as many "new age" workshops and events as possible, to see if I could find any solution to my heightened awareness that had blown my mind some years before, when a dear relative died. So, here I was a little anxious and so curious of

this initiation that we in the group waited for. What would happen? Would my life change? Did I have to become so "holy" as some of my weekend friends seemed to be? Many thoughts and a lot of deep breathing and so the moment arrived for me to enter the room where it all would take place...

It blew my head off!

It was like entering the world championship of fireworks, the difference was that it took place within me and I knew in my whole being that this was it, this was what I was born to do. My life would change dramatically, and I was on the roller-coaster without any chauffeur (at least none that I could see). I was to dedicate my life to healing, to energy work and everything else that came with it. And so my life took a sharp curve and for the next four years I was in constant training and work. I received all levels of Reiki within 6 months and then I had to learn how to compose, teach, make room for, channel energy, and ground this force of life that was everywhere within me and outside of me. I have from then on, entered many schools of healing, received initiations, transmissions, downloads, uploads and more. I have no teacher's but my Source. I have been fortunate to meet a few that have held me in their arms and space, while I have been exploring and collecting more of my "Me". And then we have "life", the greatest of teachers, maybe not the funniest at times, but constant never-the-less.

Please approach this book with an open mind and a big heart. Keep your awareness and always, always use your wisdom and knowledge to release the most of your potential.

CONTENTS

CHAPTER 1   1

A KEY INTO AWARENESS

THE KEY TO YOUR AWARENESS   2
HIGHER SELF   4
THE POWER OF THOUGHTS AND ILLUSIONS   5
HOW CONSCIOUS ARE YOU OF YOUR THOUGHTS?   6
MAKING A WISH   6
LET THERE BE LIGHT!   6
APPRECIATION OR OFFERING?   7
MY UNDERSTANDING ABOUT THE DIFFERENCE BETWEEN OFFERING AND APPRECIATION.   8
FORGIVENESS AND THE ABILITY TO FORGET   8
WHAT IS A PSYCHIC?   9
WHAT THEN IS A MEDIUM?   10
WHAT IS THE DIFFERENCE BETWEEN A PSYCHIC AND A MEDIUM?   10
INITIATION, DOWNLOAD, UPLOAD, BEING GRACED BY THE...   11
INITIATION   11
IS THIS NECESSARY?   11
DOWNLOAD   12
INTUITION   13
COMMUNICATION   14
THE ART OF LISTENING AND USING YOUR PERCEPTION ABILITIES   15
THESE QUESTIONS MAY GIVE YOU AN INSIGHT ABOUT YOUR OWN SKILLS IN THIS AREA;   16
CONFLICTS   16
TAKE A MOMENT AND FEEL HOW YOU REACT TO WHAT IS WRITTEN BELOW   17
FREEDOM   17
WHAT SIGNIFIES DARKNESS   17
RESISTANCE OR SURRENDER   18
HEART EXPANSION   19
DOES OUR WILL ARISE FROM THE HEART   20

HOW TO DEVELOP YOUR AWARENESS

The white fire (transformative)	23
Your creation arises from your brain	24
To visualize	25
Mind follows intention	26
Three examples for practicing your mind	26
The garden	26
The bus driver	26
The letter	27
To see with one's eyes closed	27
Visualization using Breathing as a tool	28
Communication	29
Words that can carry you on	29
Words – expressions	30
To follow your body towards the feeling of Expansion	31
The answer!	32
how to Merge with your heart	32
Dreams	33
Physical body awareness, interpreting your dream	34
Expansion	35
a quick way to clean and transform your own energies	36
To Strengthen Your Own Energy	36
Exercises in Returning and exchanging energy	37
Create and recreate balance in your body and mind	39
Create your own space with and from your heart	40
Protection – to shield / embrace oneself	41
Meditation / Ceremony	42
Out in restaurants or any other public area	42
Responsibility	42
Standing in a queue	43
Sleeping	43
The curtain	43
Meditation to create good flow	43

Upgrade the environment you are spending time in 44

The art of cleaning 45

These are my suggestions and thoughts about keeping a house clean 45

How to balance yourself with a quick and easy method 46

Words your body may vibrate in tune with 47

Organ 48

Negative 48

Positive 48

The grid of Light 49

Free your inner Light 49

Socks 50

A body part 50

An object 50

Person to Person 50

reflections 51

Actions! 51

Healing! 51

Safety! 51

Fear! 51

Love! 52

To play and explore with a partner 52

To pull down the rainbow 53

Chakra readings with fabrics 53

Drawing the auric fields 54

The mirror 54

To share spinal energy 54

You are my beloved 55

CHAPTER 3

57

TOOLS

The tools 58

Voice 59

Breath 59

Hands 59

Feather 59
Rattle 59
Stick 60
Stones 60
Essences 60
Incense 60
Bags 60
To start your dance with the Stone people 62
Encoding the stones 63
Crystal Waters are a good way to get access to the crystal's power. 64
Way to go 65
A little history about flower essences 65
The history 66
Water holds memories 66
Essences can be used several ways 67
The skin 67
The bath 68
Body Spray 68
Room Spray 68
How to make your own essences 68
Elements 69
Wind 71
Water 71
Fire 71
Earth 71
How to integrate the elements 71
The (medicine) wheel of transformation 72
South – the direction of my past 73
West – the direction of my dreams 73
North – the direction of my wisdom 74
East – the directions of my home 74
Adding the elements into the wheel 74
Explore the wheel of transformation 75
Cast a circle 76
Pendant or Pendulum 77
Cleansing with feathers & sage or similar incense 78
To clean the energies out of a room 79
Creating your own altar 80
a little fun in the importance of colours 81

Red wisdom   81

Orange wisdom   82

Yellow Wisdom   82

Green wisdom   82

Turquoise wisdom   82

Blue wisdom   83

Indigo wisdom   83

Violet wisdom   83

Mantra, using your voice   83

My story of the word mantra   84

Sound and chanting to your chakras   86

Sound balancing   87

geometrical forms and healing vibrations   88

CHAPTER 4   91

THE BODY

The body   92

Daily self care   94

How do emotions affect our Body   94

The belt and the plug   95

Locating the core in your body   96

A balancing and strengthening meditation for your right and left halves of your brain   97

The connective tissue   98

The lymphatic system   98

trapped in a web   99

Assemble your energy in a quick and powerfilled exercise   100

Dna meditation   101

The aura or what dances around our bodies   102

Our seven subtle bodies   103

Etheric body   103

Emotional body   103

Astral body   104

Soul body   105

Spiritual body   105

Play your own melody 106
Form a closed circuit 107
See the colors in the aura 109
Here are suggestions of a colour interpretation 110
Working with another person 112
Aura cleansing 112
How to measure and balance the auric field 113
How to Scan a body 113
To Receive a gift from your higher self 114
Meditation of the Blue flame 115
Breathing a way of living 116
Long deep breathing 117
Ssss-exercise 118
Breathing exercise for focus and grounding 118
Breath of fire 119
Alternate nostril breathing for balance 119
Breathing that clears your blood and revitalizes you with four sets of breathing tecniques 120
1st round 120
2nd round 120
3rd round 121
4th round 121
Breathing & Visualization 121
Colour breathing 122
A balancing breath to harmonise the brain 124
The chakra system-your seven energy centres 124
The chakras can be defined like this 126
1 Independence 126
2 Strong self-image 126
3 Confidence 127
4 Generosity 127
5 Safety 127
6 Overview 127
7 Leadership 128
Balancing the chakras by using toning 128
Hoola hooping through your chakras 129
Exercise & mantra sat kriya and sat nam 129
balance yourself with quick and easy method using crystal energy 130
Basic chakra balancing 131
Chakra balancing by releasing debris from the auric field 133

Rainbow visualization 134
Meridians 134
To enhance the flow of your meridians in a yin yogalike exercise 136
To release blocked energy in the meridians 140
The Five elements healing, using a crystal 140

CHAPTER 5 143

HEALING

Take good care of yourself and the energy you create 144
Imagine this about your daily energy resource. 144
What do you usually do? 145
What could you have done to ease up this daily chaos? 145
About healing yourself 146
Breathing with intention using the Unified Chakra breath 146
Meditate 146
Reflections 147
Daily life symbolisms 147
The Body 147
Dream and Meditation diary 148
Action 148
My Body Feels Congested And Needs A Release 148
The Sieve 148
The Rake 149
Distance and self healing using your knees 149
Self healing using your knees 150
Healing crisis 151
To create and restore the balance within; on a physical, emotional and spiritual level 152
Sometimes we need to just re-calibrate ourselves 152
increase of frequency 153
Energy boosting 154
Meditation the Bubble of harmony 155

MEDITATION

Meditation	158
Breathing	158
Benefits of meditation	159
Health Benefits	159
Control Your Own Thoughts	159
Detachment	159
Happiness and Peace of Mind	159
Spontaneity and Creativity	160
Discovering Your Life Purpose	160
Basic meditation	160
Meditation to create good flow during the day	161
Meditate over a cup of tea	162
Spiral Meditation	162
Earth light meets sky light	163
The Angel Meditation (Around A Corner)	164
Your inner woman and man merging	165
Parallel lives	167
The balloon	168
Heart temple	169
Rainbow Beach Meditation	171
Your Divine Image	172

CHAPTER 1

A KEY INTO AWARENESS

THE KEY TO YOUR AWARENESS

For me awareness is the foundation of one's path. When you embrace the energy of awareness you are opening the doors of your consciousness and can start to connect deeper into yourself. My aim is to present various items for you that will open up your awareness and expand your senses, make you curious and send you off on your own path through this book.

What better topic to start to talk about than the topic about guides. A guide in this context can be described as a feeling of a presence. This presence will sometimes take an etheric form so we can perceive and make ourselves a picture of its gender, age, clothes etc. If you attend a healing workshop or any other workshop where you are working with expanding your senses you will most certainly come across the question about guides. So what is a guide? Where will I find my guide? And how do I work with them?

My view of guides has changed over the years. Since childhood one strong connection I have always felt was to the "One" source. He is like how I would have wanted a grandfather to be. He is my family and I have acted out with him as if he is of flesh and blood since childhood (mild tantrums and so). Once in my home in Peru, a friend of mine came by for tea and when I opened the door to welcome her, her immediate question was "Who pissed you off, wow?" and I pointed upward to the sky. She looked at me with a curious look on her face and when she realized what I meant she cracked up completely and said that I looked and behaved as if I was five. She wondered how long I would behave like that. I said until I am not pissed off anymore and me and my grandfather have come to an understanding yeah, yeah I should know better at my age, but he is my family and sometimes I get really upset with him.

Having this strong connection of having an etheric family around me, a true source where my full trust is anchored, I was curious of all the other presences I sensed around me. Were they guides? When I channelled the voices in my head they materialized themselves. One called himself Erik and he was an old ordinary man that gave me guidance on how to interact with male authorities.

Was he possibly a guide or was he an old part of me that popped up and wanted to be released, maybe fractions of old vibrations I held within?

In my meditations I seemed to walk on a staircase and there were little alcoves where my guide for the week, day, month sat and gave me advice, reassurance, and support when needed, and when they were done teaching me, I had no access to the alcove anymore and they just waved their hands and said "move along we are done." I didn't think much about it, so I moved on.

When Reiki came into my life I certainly had a connection with that energy. Wow. They, the Reiki guides, were impressive and very helpful. I clearly felt that they were not part of "my family" the way Erik was. They fitted more into the description of guides that I had been given and read about. I made an effort to go outside my "family comfort zone" and seek them out and called in angels, devas that felt good in that moment. With them I absolutely felt a presence outside of me. Were they the guides, books, teachers and other spiritual people around me talked about?

I think for me a guide is a presence that needs to feel like my family or has a specific task or connection as the Reiki guides showed. I seem to be a little tense around a presence I don't feel familiar to. For me there is also a distinct difference between a guide and a nature spirit. The guide would be the voice of the source of spirit. So if you feel comfortable with a direct connection to "spirit", do you need guidance?

I feel that it is important for me to know and understand who and what the guide can support me with. No, it is not a control issue. I want to learn and pay my respect towards the energies that support me. Maybe we can bond and create magic together…

When I work with clients, they sometimes have an entourage with them, suddenly there is little space for me to do my work. I do not mind this at all, I always ask them, who and why they are there, sometimes it's a dead relative, a granny that is curious, sometimes it's an old source of comfort that hangs around and wants me to tell my client to let them go, for their task is done. Or, sometimes, they are old vibrations of the person that want to be embodied. It varies. There is however always a part of their source there, a Higher Self that can guide me if I feel that I get stuck in the density surrounding the body.

HIGHER SELF

One's Higher Self is an expression that is widely used in circles of people that are into exploration. It is a term that refers to a part of us that is in contact with our divinity. Some people choose to call their Higher self, their guide.

I remember my first Reiki workshop

and we started with a meditation that would connect us to our Higher selves. Our what? And when I, a little embarrassed, asked the teacher where to look for the Higher part of myself, I just received a look of sympathy and she said, you will find it when times comes. Needless to say I felt very uncomfortable and rebellious.

Today I call my Higher self the better part of me, meaning that She knows, she is not interested in any bullshit and won't please me to make me happy …

So how do you know that you are in contact with your Higher Self or someone else's Higher aspect of themselves? My suggestion is to start having a true connection with yourself and practice holding on to your faith in what you perceive.

A Higher Self's interest is to move you forward and make you understand how shifts can be done within you in the best possible way. When you have established a connection of a presence that you have absolute trust in, then you can start connecting to other people's Higher Selves as well, using the same methods you have worked out for connecting to your own Higher Self.

My experience with my Higher Self is that I will be shown pictures, I will feel feelings, I will remember things that have happened in the past, to give me a wink of how to move forward in the particular situation. This is how messages occur for me when I am working with other people as well. The challenge is to interpret and make sense of the messages and not let our own emotions pass through the interpretation. Always seek the feeling of a bodily expansion when asking a question from your Higher Self. If it feels like our body is shrinking or are indifferent, take another route. Remember mind follows intention. What you give is what you get. If you work with somebody my suggestion is to let them experience what they need to. Never take away someone else's opportunity to practice the chance to stand in their own power. They have created the situation all by themselves and should own it fully!

Beingness attracts beingness is a quote I received in the beginning of my path. I liked it then and like it now. It makes me reflect and think about what I am doing and where I am heading. For me this means that you will be guided to search, seek your own connection with your source, your guides, your Higher Self, the elemental spirits etc…

When walking on one's path, weaving one's dreams and desires for a more fulfilled life, doing one's best to support oneself and others, you attract the energies that are most helpful in the Now. If you radiate bliss and grace you will attract more of these energies and joyfully dance in this vibration. If you need to work on frustration, you will certainly be guided in this. It can be nature spirits that make you trip over hidden roots, repeatedly until you scream out your frustration towards the forest and then when you are done, realize that it is time to give grace to the nature for aiding you. So if you seem to attract a lot of negativity around you, take time and connect to your Higher Self, and ask for guidance and be open to who may appear in front of you.

Now when the time has arrived for you to seek out your personal guidance, keep your intention clear. What and why do you need to interact with guides? The more you know the easier it will be for you to select the ones that you will dance well with, where the interaction is mutual and the foundation is respect. There are still spirits that are seeking their way home and might think you are the answer to their prayers. If you feel comfortable supporting this journey, do not hesitate, it is beautiful, but maybe that was not what you intended. Never feel that you are beneath the energy that approaches you. You are supposed to merge and work together. Sometimes they want to learn from a human perspective, to be of a greater service and vice versa, it is an interaction arising from respect, willingness and love.

If you like to be in the nature, call upon the nature spirits.
If you are dedicated to a certain module of techniques, like Reiki, call upon them.
If you feel connected to the arch angels, connect and get to know their qualities, there is much to explore and there are no limits…

THE POWER OF THOUGHTS AND ILLUSIONS

I have, in my total unconsciousness, not been aware of how powerful I am….
With this quote I want to emphasize the importance of keeping a high awareness of how influential your mind is. Your mind is a powerful tool that follows your intention (purpose, goal, end, aim), your thoughts, your emotions, and signals from this intent are waltzing in and out of your body at all times. It is good to keep aware of how you use and act upon your thoughts.

How conscious are you of your thoughts?

The illusion cannot create on its own. But since "the thought" believes it can, the illusion becomes reality. To not let the illusion win in the situation and stop you from receiving your intent, I suggest that you invite "a matter" (that can be adding an image to the outcome) into the creative process, admitting more aspects of reality into "the thought." By "deciding" that the whole action takes place in a beam of light will give enough indication to your body and mind, and raise the value of "the thought" and the illusion has lost its power and has to make room for more realities.

Remember the feeling of how it is to be in the flow of creation and vibration. If you feel that you get thrown out of balance, just wait for the flow to come back into balance within you and then proceed. You will soon feel that you are part of a much larger flow, a flow always available, curious, that awaits any opportunity to manifest and form a future held in light and less density.
Creation doesn't know the word "restrictions", and have one common denominator - The Light and that All is One, mixed in perfect harmony…

Making a wish

I have many times randomly made a wish, and they were seldom returned. I paid so much attention to what I wished for, believing they would not come into reality anyway. After an incident with a wish I made for myself to become lighter, which ended up me being unable to eat solid food and having to call my sister for help to trace my mistake, I am now much more inclined to truly be aware of what I wish for and to hold my intention clearer.
Usually when we make wishes we carry a longing, a desire, a hope that all will be good now. My suggestion is that you clearly state your purpose, where and to whom you are dedicating your wish, your attention and your love towards. Be specific about the sender (you) and the receiver, and also be clear if you are asking any guides to support the cause.
Keep your intention clear, preferably write down the words you intend to carry forth so you don't forget the words used (that happens even to the best).

Let there be light!

These are powerful words to say out loud.
Words good to use when you feel that life or a situation is getting to you. Maybe you just need a little respite to understand what's going on? Maybe you need an extra shield for some

time. Maybe you wake up in the middle of the night, uncertain of what woke you up, and got a little scared, and before your brain starts to seek for an answer, say: "Let there be Light!" *Rest in that feeling of being in the Light, it is a Divine light willing to support you.*

Prayer

One of my grandmothers always made my sister and I say a children's night prayer when we had a sleepover. Neither of us had any belief in her "God," but we have always been very efficient and prioritized being alone, so we learned this one children's prayer. I am very grateful for this prayer. It has helped me many times waking up disoriented and trying to get my body and Me back to together and calm down.

So if you have a prayer, use it.

A prayer does not mean that you have to be religious to create it. Let the words be your navigation tool. Let your intuition, your true energy, vibrate from the core of your heart, surround you, embrace you, take on the intention needed and bring you to the state of centre that you seek to make the prayer dance with your Higher-Self and be supported and followed trough.

APPRECIATION OR OFFERING?

Appreciation: the act of estimating the qualities of things and giving them their proper value as in a feeling or expression of gratitude.
Offering: something offered in worship or devotion, as to a deity; an oblation or sacrifice!

I found it difficult to know what was what. Did I use the correct word when I described my doings? Did I by any chance offend any deity by using the wrong word? When living in Peru the word offering was used a lot, and for me that seemed very religious but I learned to relax in this by getting a closer understanding about the Andean tradition. *In this tradition of the Andes, the pacos, shamans create a "despacho," as an offering to Pacha Mama (Earth) and the Apus (mountain spirits). These despachos are the foundation of this tradition and is widely used for anything that you want to bring to light. I like to create something showing my appreciation and happiness that I always feel so welcome in nature: a bundle of flowers that I arrange, stones in a formation that has a meaning for me, a feather if I feel to connect deeper to the wind, the list can be long....*

My understanding about the difference between offering and appreciation.

I was walking in the mountains searching for the place where I wanted to give my thanks for the day. I received a strong transmission the day before and carried a strong feeling of freedom within me, a feeling I had sought after for a long time. It came to mind that I was not making an offering to "leave and release anything from me that would need some universal support", as that was not the message I wanted to send out. No, I wanted to dance with the elements, I wanted them to feel my Me and the happiness that poured out of my systems. I wanted to send out joy, gratitude, shimmering lights from my heart. And that for me is to show appreciation, I wanted to give thanks and blow kisses to the Stone people and Tree people that surrounded and held me so warmly. Conclusion: When I ask for support and want to show my gratitude (for something I have received), it is an "offering" and when I just want to send bubbly energy from my Me to the nature, the Universe, a person etc, it is an "appreciation." I feel that I want to have that distinction in my life.

Take a moment and feel into the difference between these two, what you create within yourself when you want to show someone, something that you are thankful for.

FORGIVENESS AND THE ABILITY TO FORGET

For me these two actions are crucial to be able to move on in my life.

It is commonly said that we who choose to work supporting people, as healers, psychologists, priests, etc, have issues that we need to work out. I can agree that by being confronted by helping others we also help ourselves to a clearer understanding about ourselves. I am not saying it is wrong at all, it is good to be able to be more aware, and to be forced to have an objective stance in matters that we have had an issue with.

For example My source in life has from the beginning made sure to test my ability to serve without judgment, and I have known within myself, that I better get a grip of whom my clients represent to me from the beginning, otherwise I will just have a tougher task to work through it. It has been very, very challenging at times and I have cursed myself for not understanding the root cause within myself, so I can be free of this client and move on with my life. But the gratitude towards the person and myself when it all has been cleared is a reward enough to fill me with appreciation for a long time. I also find there is a lot of talk about having the ability to forgive your parents, your former partners, your ancestors, your friends etc. I would like to add that if I forgive my parents but don't let the energy be forgiven inside me, as in that I just forgive mentally but forget to add my body, I will be facing that issue again and again. For me, a shield of defence rooted, in case the incident might happen again, I am bound not to forget.

What we seem to forget is that by holding on, we have automatically reserved a space for this event to happen again, and it will happen, be sure of that. Stagnant emotions are like a virus in the body and your body will create whatever situation it can, to put you into getting the virus out of your system (release). A good saying and visualization is "life creates life" meaning that there are no shortcuts. There is only acceptance. Give yourself permission to feel, to be in the emotions, destructive as well as life filled. Have patience. Respect yourself for dealing with the issue. Give yourself permission to take the time you need to work it through. Communicate. Be honest with what you experience, if there is another person involved, also respect the other person's point of view. You don't have to understand but you need to respect that your opinions differ, don't have expectations, neither of yourself or the other. There are no shortcuts. What will help you move forward is Honesty and Gratitude. Love to life, and then freedom to weave your path with a clear intention and clear heart energy.

WHAT IS A PSYCHIC?

A lot in this "new age" that we are right in now, there is talk about if or how to see, to perceive, to attune your instrument to its fullest potential etc. Again I would like to point out the importance of being aware and to have faith in what your body and spirit shows you.

I have been asked this question several times "are you a psychic?"
How would I know?
Since childhood I have always "known and perceived" motions, feelings, flows around me. I have today built a language of how to interpret what I perceive, not letting my ego stand on stage and show off. I have allowed dead people to come through my body, making me shrink back into a tiny Ewa inside of my body. Usually this happened when I have had a client in great distress because of a near death. I remember the first time it happened. A woman whose brother just passed over was devastated and somehow felt that she had not been there enough for him. Anyway, I "left" or shrunk and suddenly I felt myself become a man. That was a shock to my system. Wow, such a different energy, metabolism, heavy, manly… and I had an organ. That was the weirdest thing: something that made my crotch stretch downwards. He managed to embrace his sister and by sending these physical feelings of love, comfort and assurance that all was good, she eventually calmed her senses down and I could return into my full body and continue doing my work. I have

let myself be a channel for spirits on other occasions as well. I believe that if I tap into a vibration that I am comfortable with; I can be a "spokeswoman" for this spirit.

A psychic, for me is any individual who is sufficiently sensitive to react to psychic influences around them, from the energy of places and people, and who pays attention to their normal intuitive awareness. Some people do this more than others as their intuitive ability is more marked. By constantly registering such reactions, the sensitive person learns to discern his/her reactions to a more refined extent. The brain learns to "interpret" the incoming signals of information as waves of energy.

A psychic is not necessarily a medium, though every medium is naturally psychic.

What then is a medium?

A far more highly sensitive individual, whose heightened sense of awareness can be used to form links between the dead and the living, i.e. between the spirits of the departed wanting to communicate with friends and loved ones that still reside in physical form on earth. There are variations of how you communicate with the spirits and how the information is given out. Sometimes the spirit "takes" over the body, you become them, you can change your voice, your facial expressions, your attitude and the way you normally hold your body posture. Or you simply "hear" the message and pass it on.

What is the difference between a psychic and a medium?

The psychics, whether conscious of it or not, receive or draw their information from the living vibrations of energy around them, on earthly levels. The mediums, mostly unconsciously at first and later deliberately, adjust their level of consciousness, paying acute attention mentally to higher, faster vibrations of energy. By doing so, they receive information from sources outside the customary normal communications levels used by humankind. It is rather like tuning from MW to VHF on the radio tuner. The medium changes mental consciousness-frequency so that, when attuned, communication received from the spirit world can be passed on verbally. The medium then becomes a receiving and transmitting station. As with a TV-set the instrument, that is, the medium, has to learn how to control the frequency in use, in order to maintain control of any possible "atmospheric" interference of any kind.

INITIATION, DOWNLOAD, UPLOAD, BEING GRACED BY THE...

What do all of these words mean?

What does it matter to me?

Do I have to receive these to continue on my path, or…?

In the beginning of my own path of awareness and when I let my curiosity take over and I started to attend as many workshops as possible, hanging around drinking tea at spiritual cafés, seeping in this very interesting life that was happening around me, I always heard people talking about how strong their downloads had been the day before, or how good this teacher was in giving initiations etc. I was very curious by all of these talks and tried to understand. When I attended my first Reiki workshop my initiation was massive, it felt like my head expanded and would never go back to its normal size again. I received downloads all weekend during the meditations we sat through. I had instant "know-how's" and insight about that being a healer and being of service was my next step in life. I got more than I ever expected. And after that, downloads and uploads are like a constant part of my life.

Initiation

I have never read any documentation about how an initiation is being scientifically performed and that is also one of the criticisms of the act, is it for real or not? I have however perceived it, performed it and seen it being done upon others. I would describe it as an energy transmission where the whole body of the initiate is being penetrated and embraced by light. This is a very beautiful and sacred act for me.

Searching for an explanation about what an initiation is, these were some of the descriptions I found. Initiation is a rite of passage, a ceremony, where you make an entrance as being accepted by a group or society. It can also signify a transformation, in which the initiate is "reborn" entering a new phase in life, a new beginning. In some traditions such as Reiki, an initiation is one of the basic modules and that is also what differs that method to many other healing methods.

Is this necessary?

I don't think it is, it will however most likely align your body and mind into a structure based upon the belief system the initiation holds. In Reiki there is an absolute connection to its energy. Each Reiki symbol that you receive holds an energy structure that has its specific

meaning and there lies strength in that, it is like you are being tapped into the Reiki realm...
In our bodies we carry our energy points, activating these will enhance the swirl of energy to be more profound and it can also help you over the "threshold". It is easier to believe in oneself, if your hands are tingling and your senses feel more vivid and sparkly. The more you practice to release energy, to connect to other people's energy bodies the easier it will flow in and out of you. Once your channels of energy have been opened they will not close. Getting a booster is a common word and act as well. This means that you will be reactivated in for example Reiki, like if you hadn't practiced for some years and wanted to feel the energy more flowing again.

I believe that practice is the one and only thing to do, to achieve the level you are aiming for. Remember we All receive our powers the same way through, our own source

Download

A download is best described as receiving an energy transmission coming from above you, it usually enters your head and travels down in your body. Upload would be the opposite. You receive a transmission coming from below you, and around you. Earth is filling you up from below. There is no saying if any way is better or stronger than the other.
I sometimes get a transmission from both Up and down and when it meets and balances in my heart area, I explode into a light that fills the entire Me and keeps me very stable and balanced.

To receive a download is similar to an initiation, the feeling of being embraced and penetrated by light. It usually occurs after you have done a big release as in opened up space within you so new energies can come into fill the void. It is like your energetic body has a hunger after new pure energy and once it has got the taste of the interaction between release and refill, you are well into the process. Remember that you will never receive a stronger dose of light than your body can process, even if at times it can feel a little unbearable...
Our physical body is the part of our constitution that needs to be fully committed to release, if it's not, there will be some sort of constipation on some level. So a download of a mental cleanse can take place month after the actual event took place.
Also what I have realized is that my body works after the structure of three. If I am doing a liver cleanse, it cleanses on three levels. Body, Soul and Spirit and that means that I will receive three downloads one for each part, and the time frame usually differs, it all depends how strong my physical body part is for that particular essence of assimilation.

Usually grace is a word that takes place in a religious environment or a description of elegance, beauty of form, manner, motion, or action. I believe that my source is the part of me that actually knows me and what's going on with me, beside me, around me and it is connected to a bigger Source where I am in harmony with the universe in its whole, this is where I am being taken when I need to be blessed and in comfort. For me being touched by grace is just when I have felt alone, life has been in turmoil and I have lost faith in what I do. In these moments I am being filled with this light that seems to know me so well, carries nothing more than softness, hope, sincerity and it makes me trusting that "it will all be okay again"

INTUITION

The word intuition comes from the Latin intueri, meaning bystander, watching or watch. Intuition is the ability to form an instant opinion or make an immediate assessment without (knowingly) having access to all the facts, and is often contrary to reason and logical understanding. In philosophy intuition can mean an inspiration, an immediate, but lively perception, preferably of the unseen. It is also used every day for omens or capricious whims... Intuition is one of the most common words when you step into the world of the "un-seen". *I remember that one of the first questions I got attending a workshop was "how is your intuition?" I had no idea, I didn't even know what the question was about. I got the impression that I needed to find out, it seemed very important to "have it". I soon realized that what I was asked about was that little feeling of light bursting inside of me when I "knew" that I was on the right track with something. Next question!!*

One of the most common questions is how do I get in touch with my intuition? My answer is simple you already are and have always been. You don't have to be divine to be in touch with your intuition. Everyone is in contact with their intuition and has acted upon it more times than they ever considered. It is using your intuition with intent and to create a key that supports you in decision making for instance, that might take some time to establish.

I believe being in close contact with this sense of "knowing" is a key to your wellbeing. To guide your body and mind to trust the feeling within, so there are no doubts in your actions, is crucial when walking in the "un-seen" world. Your body needs to be told when it has made the correct assumption, when you turned to the left instead of the right. Be aware of the dance you dance with yourself and don't hesitate to tell yourself that you made the correct turn, that is one way of establishing the connection and create a bridge between the "seen" and the "un-seen". I have poor night vision, so when I was on my way by car to my house in the countryside at night, I used to "send" out my sensory system. I pretended it was like a flying bird ahead of my car to give me an indication if there was something ahead of me that needed me to be more alert. There were always a lot of animals at night and crashing into a deer was nothing I was looking forward to. And after I had told and trained my body to feel what our "night bird" indicated, it was so joyful to drive at night.

So create what you need, how you want to feel and how you want to act upon your endeavour to become One with your intuition skill.

COMMUNICATION

The "mind" of man refers to the aspects of intellect
and consciousness manifested as combinations
of thought, perception, memory, emotion, will and imagination, including all
of the brain's conscious and unconscious cognitive (mechanisms underlying human thought processes). Subjectively, it proves the mind is like a stream of consciousness. The mind is usually synonymous with the idea of those private conversations we have with ourselves "in our heads." One of the most distinguishing characteristics of the mind is the sense that it is a private sphere no one but the owner has access to. No one else can know what is going on within us. People can only interpret what we consciously or unconsciously
communicate or express.

Body language gives us important information about a person. By getting to know your own body language you can easily understand others. Studies have shown that our verbal communication is only about 3-10% of our total communication. This means more than 90% of communication is non-verbal! It is said that the human mind has the ability to think 750 words per minute, but we only express 150 words per minute in a conversation. What happens to the rest of the 600 words? An interesting thought! Are these extra words what we express through our body language? Or do they just disappear somewhere?

Communication is the most important thing for me in interaction with other people and other aspects of myself. The power of true communication is what has brought me forth on this journey and what I constantly have to work with. I remember when I started as a therapist and I was working on a health event, giving healing sessions. I told a woman that she had what I thought looked like a sponge in her tummy, my interpretation was that she took on other people's problems *like a sponge, her interpretation was that she had Candida. I learned my lesson. In the beginning of my journey of awareness (I am still enrolled), I asked myself these questions, they seemed to help me clear my mind and move me on to the next challenge. The questions are as follows; in what areas am I strong in my communication and how does my "non-verbal" communication express itself? What do I need to improve in my communication skills? Do I need any support in becoming a more confident communicator? And as always it boiled down to what I was always being shown. It is all about the return energy and the exchange of energy, and the interpretation.*

Food for thought!

∂   I am the one who chooses what mood I am expressing

∂   I am the one who chooses to take or not take responsibility

∂   I am the one who chooses to follow the energy sprung out of discomfort

∂   I am the one chooses the desire for change

∂   I am the one who chooses to have a loving attitude

∂   I am the one who chooses to be neutral in a situation and not get personal

∂   Sometimes consciously choosing to agree to disagree may be the key to respect towards myself and others.

THE ART OF LISTENING AND USING YOUR PERCEPTION ABILITIES

How do I truly know that what I heard really is what that person meant? I have always thought of myself as being a great listener. I have however re-defined that over the years. I realized that I was not only listening, half of me was trying to come up with a solution, fixing the matter, trying to steer the person in a direction etc, etc. Today I define a good listener as a person who can listen without making any sort of comments, verbally or by sending out vibes. If I haven't been asked to have an opinion or help to find a solution, I just listen without conditions and can by that give more of me to that person. I have been told that it is good to talk to me because I give full attention to the person. I take that as a great compliment and really try to hold on to that, and if I somehow see myself drifting away from the conversation, well then I have to be honest with the person and say that and maybe they have to find a new fresher ear….

In all professions exists the importance of listening with all senses alert, it is beneficial for all parties. How easy it is to misjudge a situation or a person, when we don't listen properly. It is a skill to be a good listener and to be able to "hear" behind and beyond words, spoken or un-spoken. It requires patience, curiosity and having a bit of a detective vibe within.

To listen with all our senses or with our full perception is a skill most of us need to develop. If you have ever walked in a dark room with no sense of direction, you soon discover that there are more senses than just your physical eyes. Suddenly more of you are alert. Your skin will be aware of even the faintest feel of the wind. Your eyes seem to detect variations of darkness and come to the realization that darkness has its shades of greys too. Your whole body feels more awakened in a different way than before. It is a skill to keep all these senses alert and awakened during a conversation. It will require some patience on your behalf, but I can promise you that there is so much enjoyment in finding out more of your potential and all that you will require from this. If you are working a lot with energy awareness, do not be surprised if you start feeling and thinking as the person you are having in front of you. For some this is really awkward and for some it's what makes them really good in interacting with others.

These questions may give you an insight about your own skills in this area;

∂   Which of your senses do you observe awakening within you, when you meet people (clearer sight, hearing in between the words, touch, smell, taste)?
∂   In what specific situation does your intuitive sense usually appear?
∂   Are there any specific situations where you have no doubts about your intuition?
∂   Are you aware of when you are projecting an emotion onto someone else?
∂   How do you know when your sense is being reflected by a nearby person and does not belong to you?
∂   How do you listen with all your senses?
∂   What do you define as the difference between listening and hearing?
∂   How do you know that you actually understood what the person told you?

CONFLICTS

Are you willing to sacrifice what it takes to be in your truth?

I believe that conflicts are given to me as a wake-up call and the sooner I get into the solving of it, the better off I am and can move on with my life. I usually get really upset with myself when I end up in these situations, but have learned to just accept that it is a way of getting to know myself better and be in my truth. And it has taught me a lot about my own interactions, my co-dependency, my stubbornness and unwillingness to change, oops…

Take a moment and feel how you react to what is written below

∂ Conflict gives energy.

∂ What you focus upon seems to grow.

∂ Conflict is contagious.

∂ Conflict lives and grows.

∂ Conflict demands resources such as time and money.

∂ It takes more strength and power to live with a conflict than to deal with it.

∂ Conflicts have a tendency to involve more people than only the ones having the issue.

∂ We all have different ways of reacting to conflict, fear, anger, frustration, apathy, stress, denial and more. What is your way?

FREEDOM

Freedom for me is what I aim for in all that I do. When I was younger freedom was having my own place and care for myself. It later on became the freedom of choosing what work I wanted to perform and with whom. My freedom feeling was very much based in action. Today feeling free is the total opposite, being able to just hang around a rock watching the sun set, walking in my pace and talk to the tree people, or just be in bed all day and do as little as possible…

Taste these statements and feel into your freedom vibe

∂ I am leaving all behind to gain the freedom I believe I am worth…

∂ I am releasing all my co-dependency to my friends and family to be able to fill up my lungs with the taste of freedom…

∂ Can I have a my freedom and keep my well-paid job?

∂ Will I be able to give others the same unconditional freedom feeling, I require from them?

∂ Is there anything like an un-conditioned feeling of freedom?

WHAT SIGNIFIES DARKNESS

In this era of time there are many thoughts and ideas about dark and light. I never quite understood this. I have many times been told that we who are doing this work with ourselves only travel in light. What does that mean? That if I look into my darkest corners of my mind and discover parts of me that have not been aired for a long time, does that mean I am not light in my heart? For me there is no dark or light, only parts that are forgotten.

Ask yourself;

∂   How do I define darkness?
∂   How do I define lightness?
∂   What about the grey area. How do I define that?

The more light you shine upon an item, you strengthen the contour of the shadows.
No shadow is visible if you put your hand in front of the source of Light

RESISTANCE OR SURRENDER

The body is your dictionary, it knows, it shows and it acts…
For me to choose to live a life with more awareness the resistance has been about changing my emotional, spiritual, and physical belief systems and understanding how deep these roots have been present in my physical body. Understanding more of me has made me more aware of the way I choose to show the world who I am and also realizing the reactions I have received. It has taught me how to surrender and ask for support from friends, family and society.

Often when working with oneself, all of our systems will eventually go into total resistance. Your mind and your body have had enough of you and your meditations, workshops, heading towards developing a stronger energy system within, and doing all this feeling and healing. And since you have chosen a life in awareness and by doing so, I presume that you are a persistent person and won't stop something you really enjoy and develop from. The most common way is that the body chooses to become ill (muscle ache, flu, headaches etc). I feel it is important to understand why the body is reacting the way it is and how this re-action can be prevented in the future.

My suggestion is to be true to yourself, no matter how embarrassing it might feel. Others won't see your blushing cheeks if you don't show them. Travel back in time and see if there is a pattern to be detected. Meditate, be extra alert to what life in general is showing you, ask yourself questions like;

∂   Have I always reacted this way in this situation?
∂   What aspect of me is acting this out?
∂   How old were I when I first reacted like this?

∂   Have I made any strong decisions lately (changing career, partner, have a child, become a vegetarian)?

∂   Is all of this mine or am I being co-dependent to having these feelings? If so, to whom?

When life has presented the reason to me, I can begin my release of the cores that hold me in this situation, so I can move forward, turn the knowledge into wisdom and truly embrace the message being given to me. Even though the message can be embarrassing, it might even show an aspect of you that isn't so flattering, it doesn't matter. This is a part of you that others have noticed and by acknowledging this side, you will never lose your power again. When we own what is happening, there is not much that can take that core away from you and make you unstable again. You will remain in your truth and that makes you more willing to step into your true power and be a model for others, to give them the courage to stand in their truth…

HEART EXPANSION

I would like to end this first chapter and talk a little about our heart and its expansion.
When the heart expands after being through deep emotions, a feeling of freedom may radiate out. This feeling of freedom can easily be mixed up with a feeling of wanting to expand as in "I want a new job," or "I want out of this relationship," etc. I think that it is the rush of locked up emotions that makes us feel that we need to change and change NOW! Give change some thought. What does it mean for you and how do you usually approach change in your life? I also believe that when we release ourselves from stagnate energy, the feeling of being spacious within rises to the surface of our beings. Can it be that these moves turn into a feeling of wanting to explore? Travel is the easiest way to explore, isn't it?
Does it have to be that the travel is "outside" one's own body or can it be that we undertake a deeper travel within?
When my Heart expands, I have realized that my body reacts by wanting to travel, to explore and to feel free from boundaries. So my own conclusion is that "Freedom of Heart" for me is
the anchor of my feeling of Freedom. By knowing this and understanding that the feeling of expansion doesn't have to mean that I have to move, I welcome every moment of when I can join these two together in the same compartment so we can move towards my true destination...

m̃ba

DOES OUR WILL ARISE FROM THE HEART

The power of thy will!

This is something I have thought about. What does it actually mean and where does the will reside in the body? There are many things written about our will. How to conquer our will, how to tame our will, how to befriend our will etc, and it made me wonder if there is more than one will, as in the mind, the heart, the spirit, the soul, the work, the inherited one etc?

For me there has been a change in where my will resides, it is now residing in my heart. Before I had this energy of will residing around my navel. For many people their will resides in their solar plexus area. In martial arts and qi-gong, the power of action comes out from around their solar plexus area. Many people feel that their will acts out from their head. I believe it all depends on what one means with will and acting on one's will. For me, will is a pure energy act and it depends on the situation where it is channelled from. When I was in my teens, I carried a lot of energy and I tried to keep it within me, because when it came out, I felt like an exploding pressure cooker so I directed the energy out of my eyes, I felt it was safer. I once saw myself in a mirror when that happened and wondered who on earth could look that way and it was not until the energy started to fade that I became conscious that I was looking at myself and had a shock. I realized that I had to find a way to divert this energy some other way. I had to take responsibility for my projections so I started with various forms of body exercises.

From living my life and all of those experiences, my will now emerges from behind my heart. My heart carries intelligence and acts out from a source within me. It does not feel as physical as the other places in my body. It is much more subtle and holds a stamina that the other places don't have, at least not in my constitution. I feel that I trust more when my will acts out from my heart. It is carrying my truth and is the centre of my body. It is where all my other "wills" should have their resting place. It feels like they get back in balance quicker when they return to my heart. And there is much less motion in my heart than in my navel chakra, where the fire is ready to "go" and does not always have the heart energy tagging along. When my will decided to start acting out from my heart, I felt good, as if I knew that now I could be trusted in my actions by my higher-self and had evolved from my teenage Me, phew....

I now consult my body from where "she" believes the energy shall emerge from. When I need to hold a lot of space quickly, my fire holds me stable in my navel area. When I need to be physically strong my will dances out from my solar plexus and aids the place within that needs some support. When I need a quick solution, my will from my head keeps me alert for the time required. I am grateful for my fire, it has kept me safe, warmed both me and others, but I feel that it is an easy way to lose some of my life force and I might need that energy for other more important issues in life.

mba

Take some time and reflect over these questions

∂   Honour yourself with a moment in stillness, connect to your body and ask how many centres of will you carry?
∂   Are they in harmony with each other?
∂   Do they have their resting place within your heart?
∂   Ask your body on how to use this fantastic resource of energy the best way.

CHAPTER 2

HOW TO DEVELOP YOUR AWARENESS

In this chapter I would like you to start practicing your own awareness. In the last chapter I showed you a variety of ways in which I believe are the beginning to becoming aware. To see, feel and perceive beyond what is showing in front of you. My aim is to lead you deeper in your own abilities to stand into your own power, which I trust is extremely important when you start to open up to the infinite possibilities to evolve within and carry you forth.

THE WHITE FIRE (TRANSFORMATIVE)

I will start this chapter by introducing this wonderful tool. I am of the opinion that we need to help Earth, the Waters or wherever we are sending our energies towards after we have done a cleansing, a healing session etc. I always visualize a fire to aid me and I would love it if you found this a useful tool too.

When I started as a healer and therapist, meeting many souls in one day made me feel very unbalanced. I had not yet figured out an effective way to transform and cleanse myself off after a day from any energies that did not belong to me. As well as I was trying to balance my "old" life to a smooth transition to the path I had chosen to walk upon now. I tried to summon in helpers, even imagined I was wearing a rubber suit. I did that a lot and it was not giving me the support I needed. It brought me to the verge of questioning my new profession. "This is not how it is supposed to be," I thought. There was clearly something missing… A new day came and I had a client who I found carried very heavy energies, which I sucked in as a melting ice cream. I dreaded the meeting since I had had a night with disturbing dreams. After I had set up my table, standing there trying to figure out if I dressed myself in a double etheric rubber suit could work… my table was set on fire. I was stunned and rubbed my eyes. Nope, it was still there, full ablast in a shimmering, white colour. So beautiful and so clean. I heard the voice in my heart tell me that it was now time for me to receive a gift in the form of the white, transformative fire, to support me in my work. It shrank, fitting the size of the table, and there has been no more need for any rubber suits since this day when I received my white transformative fire. I have also during these years been able to share this fire with others and they all love it. Some of them think it is the most effective tool they have ever been given, which makes me very humble and happy. I am not in favour of letting Gaia, Mother Earth get more garbage thrown at or in her. So I always transform what I release, personally and in my profession.

I will introduce some of the ways the White Fire has chosen to help us transform and the rest is up to you and your dance with it…

To light a white fire is a way to transform what you want to clean, what you no longer wish to harbour within. It is a cleaning tool, which will support you in transforming old feelings, beliefs or other "junk" you feel you want to be freed from. What is important is your intention. Flow follows thought. What do you want to accomplish? The more focused intention you have, the more directional it is, the better results you will receive. If you have a room in your home that feels a little sticky, messy, etc, connect your heart into the core of the room, tell the room what you are about to do and why and then light up your white flame in the middle of the room and let all the energy that is bound in the room be transformed by the fire.

If there is a business meeting you can with collaboration with your friends and colleagues, decide to light a fire to transform any stress, frustration or anything else that needs to be dealt with during the meeting. This also goes with group work. Make all of the members of the group connect to the white fire with their hearts. Together you light it up and ask it to transform the energies you will release. If you feel tired, stressed, sad, angry, not in balance, you can usually go in and place yourself in the fire and ask that all energies that no longer serve you be transformed.

If you travel and dread sleeping in hotel beds, where a lot of energies have been dumped, imagine a fire that transforms all of this. If it is really dense, I imagine the fire taking form as a covered sheet, which I lay upon. If you are having a guest, out of courtesy a nice gesture is to light a fire so they can be allowed to be in their space in the room. There is no limit on how to interact, use, and dance with this tool of pure Light. Meditate with it, start your own dance and ask how it can support you in your life. Always have your heart connected. It symbolizes that you take full responsibility for your actions. Remember this is a sacred key into understanding your own power and shall be appreciated as this.

YOUR CREATION ARISES FROM YOUR BRAIN

I love my brain, its simplicity mixed with the un-known possibilities it has shown me over the years. As upset as I can be with my brain, when it is not letting go of an old belief system or feeling I have worked with, I have to admire it for forcing me to go deeper within and find new ways of letting go. I somehow have to admire the energy behind it and I think I can be quite tiresome to deal with sometimes...

Your Brain is a very delicate instrument. It holds All and nothing, which in my opinion makes it unique and fun to play with. Yes the brain loves to play, it's the best playmate you can have, and you just have to be in-tune so you are playing the same game. Your Brain needs good direction to act its best. Your Brain cannot perceive if an event is happening now or if it's old, it is up to you to tell it. Your Brain stores memories. It's an encyclopaedia of all your past and present emotions and experiences. Your Brain can hold on to a thought form, a mind worm, until you have somehow persuaded it that a new thought is better, and that the brain will gain from releasing this mind worm. The Brain has its own form of logic. Understanding this logic can help you move out of your comfort zone and see an issue from a new perspective. The Brain loves attention. If you have constantly fed it attention and suddenly stop, it is like having a spoiled child screaming and doing everything to get your attention back. Remember that Mind follows intention in emotional, mental and physical ways. The brain will behave guided by what you feed it. As I said, it loves to play. Visualization is one way of playing. If you create a picture in your mind the Brain does not distinguish between that and an actual event. If you create a picture in your morning mediation of you having a successful presentation at work, you will simply walk into the meeting and be the success you have already been.

TO VISUALIZE

Being a "highly sensitive" person, I have always being showered with images, or being presented an image with a feeling attached to it. For me visualization has been crucial to develop in a much deeper way, so I could be the master of the situation I am in and not the energy that has come with it. It took me years to develop enough skill to be able to hold my visualization during hours of meditation for instance. I took courage to stick to what I was being presented with and to work and accept this. I took time for me to truly enjoy the ride and not feel lost in all of the images and emotions. Now I love it, enjoy it and travel well with it.

When you visualize you create an intention, a mental picture of something you want to happen or something that has already happened, with this you involve and create with all your senses. To visualize means that you see/create the images, with your "inner eyes", but you will also use more than just your inner eyes, you will see as well as connect all your other senses to make it as persistent as possible. To perceive, means that you become aware of, or identify with the support of your senses, hearing, feeling etc. When the images are taken from your own memory, they are more powerful than if someone is giving you the images to work with (as in a guided meditation). If you do not have a memory, create one...

Mind follows intention

The more intention, vivid pictures, and movement associated with the image, the stronger signals you send to your brain that this is "for real". It can be something you would like to happen, or to alter and transform something that has already occurred, as in something you would like to change the outcome of. This is what meditation can support you with. The stronger your intention is, as in the more you "believe" in that this will actually occur, that it is possible for it to occur, the stronger flow of energy you will receive and then most probably feel, and or perceive the event stronger in your body. The stronger flow that is created within you, the better your result will be. The more evocative your image is, the more your senses will be able to act upon the image. If you imagine that you are in a relaxed state, you give your brain a signal that you actually are in this state (this is the beauty of your brain, it trusts you, so give it an accurate picture).

Three examples for practicing your mind

The garden

Imagine that you are having a stroll in the garden of your childhood. Your brain will be activated and remember what your favourite flowers were, your special corner and how the wind rustled through your hair. Enjoy the moment, the scent of the flowers, breathe in deeply, feel how you stand barefoot in the grass. Add the songs of the birds and the sound of a little creek, and you have created a complete visualization. For the best effect let the pictures be your own, it creates a different safety feeling for your body, allowing it to relax deeper and the visualization becomes more effective. This means that if you are listening to a guided meditation and the person talking says to see all the lilies in the garden and your garden had roses, not lilies, well do choose the roses unless it is a specific flower meditation and there is another meaning behind the flowers being visualized.

The bus driver

One day you behaved really badly on the bus, shouting at the driver because you had had a bad morning and somehow he looked like an easy target. That situation is hard to change since you don't know him. What you can do is to visualize that you stay on the bus until the end station, walk toward the driver and sincerely ask for his forgiveness, you say that it was awful letting him be the target of your stored anger, etc. Feel, see how your intent really merges with him and his body relaxes and he smiles back at you. In that moment also feel how you're body relaxes and a smile enters you as well.

The letter

If you send away a letter visualize how you would like the receiver to feel when the letter is being opened and read, like getting an open curious feeling in their heart and mind.

Once I was seeking a scholarship for a course. I had found one I wanted to attend, so the day before my meeting I sat down in meditation visualizing how the meeting would go. I saw myself sitting opposite the man in charge and I started to send energy from my heart to his brain and then to his heart over to my brain, so we would fully understand each other on a more heartfelt level, or to be honest, I needed him to understand my point of view…

Another picture emerged instead, that stunned me and I got the feeling that I really needed to pay attention. I saw a band-aid over my mouth (was I not supposed to speak?) and my ears grew big. I also had to connect my strong-willed mind to my root and of course my heart was wide open…what was this? I sat with this picture, going through all my emotions of being unable to talk, hrmmm argue for my cause, while keeping an open heart listening to what I was being told. With a curiosity I went to the meeting the following morning and I am so grateful that I was prepared. In retrospective the course he suggested (not the one I wanted to attend) gave me so much more on many levels and aspects that I couldn't have known at the time.

So be open to what comes to you.
Be open to the other parts as well.
Be open to receive guidance from your Source…

TO SEE WITH ONE'S EYES CLOSED

This is a phenomenon that can occur during deep relaxation or meditation. It's like you see through your eyelids, whilst they are still closed…it is not supposed to happen. I am not sure how scientists would explain this…

The first time it happened to me was during a meditation and I thought I had opened my eyes because I saw the door open, but then I realized that I was still in deep, deep meditation. I managed to compose myself and not open my physical eyelids and started to explore what was happening.

I looked around the room and saw the rest of the group sitting still in meditation, my teacher however must have sensed something, she stared at me and I just smiled and she looked a little puzzled. I managed to keep this perception for about 5 minutes then I guess my brain started to register that this was not the "correct" way of viewing so it demanded that I either close my eyes or open them. I retreated and went back to the ordinary way of seeing my inner world instead of the true outer one.

This usually happens to me when I am in deep relaxation or when I am being disturbed during a meditation or a journey of some sort. It is as if one part of my body wants to check what is happening around me, and does not want to bring me back to the present fully. If it happens to you, still your brain and tell it that it is okay to enjoy another way of perception…

VISUALIZATION USING BREATHING AS A TOOL

1. Sit or lay down in comfort.
2. Breathe and find your pace. Let the breath light emerge from your heart and merge with all of your etheric bodies.
3. Exhale white energy and let the energy fill up your body with the intention to expand your body.
4. Inhale and let your body expand throughout your auric field.
5. Exhale and relax, stay in the size you have created.
6. Inhale and expand one meter outside the entrance door.
7. Exhale and relax, stay out there, open your ears, what do you hear?
8. Inhale and expand into the street, what do you hear, what do you smell?
9. Exhale and relax with your senses open and curious.
10. Inhale and expand into space, what do you sense?
11. Exhale and bring the feeling of space back into your body.
12. Inhale and listen to your own insides, follow the blood streams, place yourself in the chambers of your heart.
13. Ask to be shown how your body looks from the inside
14. Keep on breathing and just float around in your sensory system for a while.
15. When you are ready, keep an intentional breath so that you slowly bring yourself back to the now.
16. Move your body a little, open your eyes and before you start to do anything else, write down how you feel, what you experienced, etc…

COMMUNICATION

For me the aim of communication is to create magic. Magic in your own life and with the ones you meet. To be aware how your communication travels in your energy field and how it touches others has been a gift and a good lesson for me. Communication is about listening, listening to yourself and to the people you meet. It is about being aware and showing respect.

1. Sit still for a few minutes and listen to the sounds around you, it can be voices, a humming from a machine, breathing or a bird. Anything...
∂ Focus on your throat and feel how this area feels. Is it tense, light, airy or thick?
∂ Roll your head softly in a circular movement clockwise and counter-clockwise to loosen up any tensions in this area. Sit still and focus again how the throat area feels. Did the rolling make the feeling change?
2. Visualize a shimmering light that emerges out from your throat.
∂ Feel how this light expands and carries the intention to become bigger and then finally surrounds all of your physical as well as your etheric bodies – your auric field.
3. Visualize this shimmering light as a free flow of communication. Wherever you direct your voice, it will expand and embrace the people you encounter throughout your day, with respect and delight.
4. Bring the shimmering light back to surround only your own bodies, bring it to the core of your heart and say to yourself:
∂ "I own all my actions of communication and aim to bring magic with these, into the communicative dance with the people I encounter."

(If you work in pairs, you can direct this energy towards each other, to feel how it is perceived.)

WORDS THAT CAN CARRY YOU ON

When you do not understand what somebody says, do not struggle to understand each word.
Stop the attempt! Silence yourself within and listen with your inner self (as in the little whispering voice that carries you forth. Some might call it intuition, guiding angels, higher self, etc.).
When you are puzzled by what you see or hear, do not try to understand. Place yourself a little on the side and be quiet for a while! When you are calm, the complicated things seem

simple to interpret. To know what happens, do not push. Open to the unexpected and be aware. See without staring. Listen quietly instead of listening intensely. *Use intuition and reflection instead of trying to figure out an answer for everything.*

WORDS – EXPRESSIONS

For me words have become an issue. The more I'm embracing awareness, the more I treasure words and try to use their true value and meaning. I can find it difficult since I have abused words for many years, maybe not intentionally, merely very unconscious and being lazy. I have however tried to really listen to what lies behind the words that are being spoken to me, and sometimes it's confusing, the people seem to say the same thing, just using different expressions. By using a different way of listening, I am also using a different way of talking, even if I still do "fall-in-between" sometimes…

The intention with this exercise is to write down words you want to reflect upon, feel through, searching for the "root sense" that will support you in your inner work and maybe send some mind worms on vacation. You are in an emotional and mind-worming state and having a hard time finding peace within, you have searched the root cause for some time and all that you are getting back is a feeling of despair, this is a method that can ease you out of your own spiral of confusion and maybe set the path on track again.

Start by thinking about these three things:

1. To connect to a true part of yourself you need to be objective and more balanced. Find your pace with your breath and body. Let your mind sink into your heart and merge to be able to receive the answers on your issue. Consider following questions;
2. What is my intention with ridding my "mind worms"?
3. What do I seek out of the answers I will come upon?
4. What is the aimed outcome?
5. Continue by writing down the words that describe how you feel. Just let the thoughts flow freely. Feel and sense each of the words, and then start sorting out the synonyms. It is very common to use similar words to describe the same issue
6. When you have reached a workable set of words let's start.
∂ Example: "not seen, not appreciated, angry, sad, emotional, untrue, locked in, not able to move ahead, tummy ache, headaches, not sexy, fat, having a hard time to forgive," and it goes on.

7. Write down a word, such as forgiveness, for example.

∂ What does this mean for you?

8. If you trace the feelings of the word forgiveness down to the root of your own interpretation does it make sense or is there a blockage within you?

∂ Is there something you refuse to be aware of or something you refuse to let go of, such as pride?

9. How far did you reach tracing your own limitations encountering this word? Are there layers left to be unfolded?

10. Where is the root of these layers anchored, mentally, physically, spiritually? Do you accept them?

11. Where can you find support to release and work these out? What do you need to do?

This is an effective, structured way of tracing issues within. If you can be truthful with yourself, this becomes a very effective way to release yourself from a self-image that no longer serves you, opening yourself to new possibilities, beyond the ones you and others have been presenting.

TO FOLLOW YOUR BODY TOWARDS THE FEELING OF EXPANSION

I trust that my body knows what it will bring forth in my life. When I might be trapped and dancing with my mind worms, my body is taking a nap and patiently (often) awaits me....
When I have danced this fruitless dance with my mind worms and just want results, my body gets my attention by whispering "follow the expansion Ewa"... This has shown to be a wonderful tool of mine, that always makes me be in my Me, takes me beyond any disbeliefs and helps me make my decisions...

1. Breathe, make yourself comfortable and set a clear intention, which is: you have full trust in what your physical body will show you and help you feel. You will either have a sense of expansion, indifference or a feeling of contraction - "shut down".

2. Visualize your issue and embody the feeling, the picture etc (for example: should I go to Majorca for vacation?).

3. When you feel that this is done, ask your body to enter a space of expansion if it thinks this is the correct choice for you.

4. Sit and breathe with your body and follow the movement, what did it say? If you don't want to believe fully what your body tells you, ask it to give you a picture of why it chose expansion.

If you are new to working with your body in this way, it would be a good idea to get accustomed to this way of trusting by sitting and practicing the feeling of yes (expansion), no (contraction) and indifference (no motion) until you feel that you and your body dance to the same tune.

THE ANSWER!

Sometimes you are stuck in your own mind worms and cannot connect to find answers, not even on simple questions. This is an easy meditation for when that happens.
It is night, visualize that you are walking on a path and the surroundings are all shimmering white. You are walking towards a house at the end of your path.
The front door is open and an inviting light is pouring out from the room just inside the door. In the room stands an altar. The objects on the altar are for you to create and support you this moment.

1. Turn around and find that in front of the window stands a chair draped in shimmering purple fabric. Place yourself in the chair and feel how you merge with the energies of the fabric, the items in your circle and your inner heart while the moonlight pours upon you.
∂ Breathe, connect, relax and be in total balance – within and without – and ask your question.
∂ If you have many questions (we tend to have that) pick out the most important one and focus on that. You might get blurry answers otherwise…
∂ Await your response, sit with the answer and let it sink in.
2. When you feel ready, rise from the chair, place the items back on the altar, give your thanks and walk out of the house.
3. Notice how the atmosphere has changed, how the white world suddenly has colours, vibrant colours. Stand for a moment and let the colours come forth and enter your heart and then merge with the rest of your body.
4. Make your way back on your path and walk back "home."

HOW TO MERGE WITH YOUR HEART

Having a bad day?
Just by being aware that your energy resources are not on top, is great. That makes you less inclined to give away the energy resources you have that day. Holding on to your resources is

sometimes crucial. Here is a suggestion what you can do before leaving your house to enter the world if you feel a little vulnerable.

1. Sit or lay in comfort
2. Breathe, make sure you feel that you are connected to the ground, spine is vibrant and head is upon your shoulders.
3. Exhale all tensions you feel your body is holding, and direct it towards the visualized White Fire (a fire meant for transformation).
4. Inhale with the intent to support your body with new energy.
5. Inhale and imagine that you place the energy of your mind into the core of your heart.
6. Exhale and let your heart energy merge and bring itself out of the heart area and surround your bodies. Continue to breathe out from your heart until you feel that you are in balance with all of your bodies.
7. Then ask your body to create the "space-you-need-for-today" with the vibration and density to keep your energy level intact throughout the day.
8. If you feel to add some extra words, colours, etc, feel free to do that.

DREAMS

I was fortunate to live in the same building as a dream interpreter during a period of time when my dreams were so vivid and crazy. I had fun, but also had a hard time making any sense of them. I asked her if there was any simple way to interpret dreams, visions and things that got presented to me in my meditations. She told me a simple and yet very powerful way to interpret that not only eased my mind but also created space for me to understand and work through what I was processing at the time. When dreams occur and we remember them when we wake up, our unconscious mind has worked through a lot and sometimes leaves us with a mess of emotions, interactions, mind worms, dreams and fears, getting us ready for a release, understanding and interaction with ourselves. Dreams are mostly about the present in that they represent things you and your body are working through now, even though they can be presented as a childhood friend that you have not seen since you were nine years old…

I dreamt about my school friend and woke up with a big question mark bouncing in my head, why did Mary occur in my dream? I got curious and created space within by breathing and expanding my body and mind, to be able to go deeper into this mystery. My first thought was what does Mary represent for me, if I would describe her for someone today, how would my interpretation be?

She was sweet and very shy, talked very low key. She was not attending the regular religion hours in school because she belonged to a church that didn't allow any other interpretation of the bible than theirs. She was a loner. I then started to think about what was going on in my life at that moment. No one has ever accused me of being low key or shy (J) however I have taken a step out of the regular "society" since I started to actively study energy medicine. Being a healer was a very suspicious profession to choose, was it not enough just to meditate and be quiet about it? I am a loner, as in that I have no problem being with Me and only Me.

So my interpretation was that my Me had taken a step forward and wanted me to be more aware, care and feel at peace with the decisions I had made. To find a way to release what has bound me to my old me and mind sets and make me aware so I could also feel when I was around "hostile" energy patterns (they felt that way at the time) that challenged me into walking with more firm steps on my re-born path. This way can also be applied to places, for example you dream of the Vatican state in Italy. Aha! The pope lives there, there is a lot of magical culture around and I do have an old dear friend there. Maybe it's time to enlighten myself with some culture, good food, hug my friend and relive some good memories and walk inside the Vatican state, maybe I even get to see the pope. Let your fantasy and curiosity about yourself guide you on the waves of dreams…

PHYSICAL BODY AWARENESS, INTERPRETING YOUR DREAM

This is a technique, where you trace the sensations your dream has left lingering within, good to use when you wake up and the dream is lingering inside you but you have no idea what it was about. If you have a diary or dream book, have it ready beside you.

1. Close your eyes again.
2. Breathe yourself back into calmness.
3. What is the feeling – sense the mood of them (the sensations). I say them because it is always more than one feeling. Do not make it complicated - I feel like I have come off a rollercoaster, I am not sure where I am, I am happy and it feels that I have accomplished something big.
4. How does your body feel – *a little nausea, sparkling, content (your body will provide you with visions, emotions, etc…)*
5. Can you sense something else – *Example; it feels like this has to do with the workshop that I will attend today and also be a part of (sometimes parallel things come to the surface that have to do with the dream but just show themselves in another reality).*

My interpretation of this would be the following; I am attending a work shop in something I am very interested in, I am assisting, I am nervous because I really want to perform and be recognized. This is a step into my New Me and I have put in a lot of energy. I really want to enjoy the day.

There are many ways of interpreting dreams. There are wonderful books about symbolism. You can use your intuition, draw a card (like a tarot card) where the text and picture might give you a hint of what is going on, there are plenty. Have fun and be creative, your body knows, it is just a matter of you daring yourself to let it guide you and trust and have faith in what it shows.

EXPANSION

Intention is to dare to expand and feel how spacious you are.
Tip! If you are in a situation where you need to make decisions and you have multiple choices in front of you, this exercise is great. Consider the choice, word, and see where the body goes into expansion…

1. Sit or lay down in comfort.
2. Breathe and find your pace. Let the breath light emerge from your heart and merge with the all of your bodies.
3. Exhale any coloured energy and let the energy fill up your body with the intention to expand your body to its fullest potential.
4. Visualize the word YES in front of you. Take a breath and inhale this word into your system and let it expand.
∂ How does it feel?
5. Visualize the word NO in front of you. Take a breath and inhale this word into your system and let it expand.
∂ How does it feel?
6. Visualize the word EXPANSION in front of you. Take a breath and inhale this word into your system and let it expand.
∂ How does it feel?
7. When you are ready, keep an intentional breath so that you slowly bring yourself back to the now. Move your body a little, open your eyes and before you start to do anything else, write down how you feel, what you experienced, etc.

A QUICK WAY TO CLEAN AND TRANSFORM YOUR OWN ENERGIES

1. Learn the Unified Chakra breathe (you will find the meditation in the chapter about healing)
2. Once you know it, it can be done in 3 minutes. It is an instant "harmoniser" which puts you back in balance and leaves you feeling strong and refreshed.
3. Clean your hands and wrists under running water, imagine that debris is leaving your body
4. Sit down.
∂ Connect to your heart and let the light within surround your bodies. Breathe in light, fresh, clear air into your heart with the intention to fill yourself with clarity
∂ Connect to Your source.
∂ Imagine a point high above your head, and imagine a shower of clear light pouring down from it, cleaning your body and your aura, reaching down to the midpoint of Earth. Or start within Gaia (another common name for Earth) and bring the light from her and up.
5. Imagine that you blow all the old, used energy out through your mouth into a big balloon. When the balloon is filled, place it in White fire to be transformed into a fertilizing light that can be used to plant with, like if you where to use it and plant a flower bed with the most exquisite flowers blossoming.
∂ Fill as many balloons as you need to.
∂ Then inhale a clear white light to your brain and let this light merge with your heart.
6. After a long day – change clothes. Clothes hold a lot of energy
7. Wash your hair, get a haircut, brush it "100-times", hair tend to hold on to energy
8. Take a quick walk.
∂ Focus on inhaling new, fresh and clear energy.
∂ Imagine the energy filling your whole system.
∂ Imagine old energy leaving you and being transformed into fresh energy by nature.
∂ If you need to - go and hug a tree or kiss some stone people or maybe even a human one

TO STRENGTHEN YOUR OWN ENERGY

This a great exercise that you can do everywhere, when you sit on a bus, in the car, on the toilet, adding to your breath exercises. This exercise balances the whole of your body, your energy centres and the organs that these correspond to. The exercise lowers your body's stress levels and makes you more focused. It is one of these great exercises that you can perform in only a few minutes after some practice.

This is a guaranteed wake-you-up exercise in the morning.

1. Find a chair, place both your feet balanced on the floor, and keep your spine and neck straight.
2. The neck is straight when it is bent slightly forward as if you were a little double-chinned.
3. Place the tip of your tongue behind the front teeth and let it rest there.
4. Breathe through your nose only, long deep breathing with a rhythmic pace, let your heart and core merge.
5. Visualize that your energy travels in a loop, start where your perineum is situated (just in front of your anus) use your breath as a tool, let it travel up through the spine, circling the head and then down through the centre of the body back to the perineum for a minimum of 5 minutes.
6. Inhale
7. Feel how the breath energy travels up from the perineum up through your spine to the head and releases any tension being held there.
8. Exhale
9. Feel how the breath energy travels around the head and then down over the face, throat, heart area, stomach, through your pelvis and back to the perineum.

Keep on travelling around with your energy breathing (feel free to add a colour or just use plain pure energy) and feel how your body is getting heavier and more relaxed and how your breath deepens. Focus on just circulating the energy around and around until your body tells you that it feels in balance and is ready for the day to come.

EXERCISES IN
RETURNING AND EXCHANGING ENERGY

To be released from old you will have to be willing to return!
I feel it is important not to carry around other people's energy in my "life", so whenever I get a chance to return and exchange lingering energy, I do. Once I had a hard time releasing myself from another person. Whatever I did (meditating, gave Reiki, sang, screamed, cried etc), it just bounced

back, and I was getting really tired of the non-fruitful dance between me and this person's energy body. Since it didn't leave me alone, I just had to find a solution. I gave it one more chance and I summoned all of my emotions towards this person, and started to go through them all, what belonged to me and what belonged to the other him. I soon realized that I had a space inside of me that was holding on to a lot of the others person's energy. I had really kept that from myself and felt that not only did I keep space within me occupied with another person's energy, I also denied the person to be in his power since I held on to his energy. What to do? I asked for guidance and was then shown these empty bottles in front of me and got an indication that they should be filled up. Aha! So I released all energy that didn't belong to me into the bottle, which I had in my mind turned into the other person's body, and then I asked the person to release all the energy that belonged to me back to "my" bottle. It took some time and I could follow the bottles being filled. When there was a little gap or a stop in the filling of the bottle, I asked to be shown (by my Higher self, intuition) where that block was in my body, or my energy points, my chakras, and realized that I was shown where our energies where still entangled. Knowing this I could then give the stop a slight intentional push to speed up the process. Finally it was done and I felt such a relief, very spacious within and was truly humble in my understanding of how and where we two had been entangled, and that we were now free to play. To be able to return someone else's power is for me essential, why would I want to keep space within me occupied with another person's energy? And it is up to me to look how deep this connection has been and where it has been the strongest and held us both from evolving. Maybe it is only me that feels stuck on a conscious level.

This method has been one of the most effective ones I have been given by my Source and I truly recommend trying it. We all have our energetic connections as in family members, friends, old partners, school mates etc. Some connections are old and worn out and need an update. Some connections are just lingering around because you forgot to tell them they could leave, and some are based upon co-dependency and need to be exchanged so you both can move forward and be in your own personal truth. In whatever area you feel you are stuck, you can use this method of exchanging. It does not always have to involve people, if you feel that you can't get yourself out of the energy of despair, make an exchange. To work with emotions this way, summon the feeling of the emotion or how you become when the emotion is as strongest within you. Sometimes it can help to visualize yourself and put that picture on the bottle. *Remember that being attached to an energy or emotion also gives you power and creates a need and somewhat of a co-dependency.*

Please modify this exercise to fit your senses and needs. We all carry our own symbols that work effectively; you have now been given the basic steps of the dance.

mba

The following exercise requires you to be honest to yourself.

It is questions that might give you some internal insights and clear some dust.
I believe that in the work one does for oneself, being honest is a must. Sometimes it's tough to admit one's own participation even for oneself, and how can we then admit it for others?

∂   Where do you sense that your carry your weak points within (mentally, physical, energetically)?
∂   Is there any reason for you to keep and/or hold onto someone else's energy?
∂   How does it serve you to do that?
∂   Do you have any vulnerable areas, which you feel the need to protect no matter what?
∂   If you tend to bring other people's energies within you, is this an act of fear or pure ego?

Think about that if you bring on another person's energy and try to transform it into yours, there is a big chance that you will miss out on your own "soul" development and purpose, being too occupied taming this new energy substitute into the same energy vibration as yours, or worse trying to enhance your own development with the help of this persons energy. Usually what happens is that you just end up having to guard this energy (since it's not yours). Soon you will be in a wheel of not being in your own truth at all, while your body is being diminished and losing its strength trying to keep up with everyone else's energy.

CREATE AND RECREATE BALANCE IN YOUR BODY AND MIND

1. Place yourself at ease and comfortably lying down on the floor. It is preferable that you wear loose-fitting clothes that do not leave any energy marks on your body, at least make sure that you have nothing that sits tight upon you like a bra, a belt etc…
2. Take a breath, center in your heart and let the light from your heart merge throughout your body.
3. Give yourself a minute to think about what you would like to add to your life (trust, joy, strength, etc.).
4. Close your eyes and turn your whole consciousness inwards.
∂   How do you feel?
∂   How does your body feel?
∂   Is your body placed with all its weight onto the floor? Is your tummy tense? Does it feel like your lower back wants to curl up, so your knees cannot be straight?
5. Let your thoughts come and leave you in a light flow.

6. Start breathing deeply, making sure that when you inhale your tummy moves from your spine and when you exhale your navel is being drawn back towards the spine.
7. Focus on your feet, let the energy of the breath spread from your soles of your feet and with awareness move it up through your legs.
8. Let your breath fill up your whole pelvis bringing with it the assigned feeling you chose, making your body open up wherever you direct your intention.
9. Let this feeling of care slowly fill up the rest of your body. Let it have its time and give you more and more feelings of ease and relaxation.
10. Let the feeling dissolve any trace of tiredness or worry that might linger within.
11. When you have filled all your body with the intended energy, rest in this space for some time and breathe through your body.
12. Then visualize your heart connecting to your spine and through all the nerves in your spine send the appropriate colour of light into every cell in your body.
13. Let the color or colours dance themselves in and around your body creating a balloon where you can release all thoughts, emotions, physical discomfort etc. Place this balloon in the White fire and let it be transformed into a fertilizing energy that can help the Earth.
14. Bring yourself and your body back into the room conscious of the floor, bring the breath into awareness.
∂   Are you in balance and at ease?
∂   How does your body feel?
∂   If there was any discomfort when you started the exercise is it now gone?
15. Breathe three times and slowly move a little, open your eyes and be here and now.

CREATE YOUR OWN SPACE WITH AND FROM YOUR HEART

The most efficient way I have discovered to bring me into my centre, give me time to re-group my energies if I feel scattered, and help me keep cleanse energies away, is to, with my intention, build a bubble of light emerging out of my heart. Since it arises from my heart, I am certain that there are no interfering energies from any other source. Why I find this way so effective is that if I draw a bubble out from my core, I will be more aware if there are energies trying to enter my body-bubble. If I am walking home and feel a little vulnerable, the bubble will keep me alert of the surroundings. If I am working really hard, unaware that I need a break, my bubble will make me aware of this, usually by getting me a little agitated at the ones around me, forcing me to take some time for a cup of tea.

1. Visualize that from the core of your heart's centre, a light starts building up until it has the density and vibration you need for today, this present moment, or whatever the reason might be. Let the light surround your etheric bodies. Since your body knows exactly how big it needs to be for the occasion addressed you can just enjoy the feeling of being embraced by a shimmering light.

2. If you want to create a picture of the size of your bubble, so you are in total comfort, visualize drawing a circle as big as your arms stretched out to your sides, straight up and behind and in front of you.

If you find that you have forgotten to create your bubble for the day, just find a spot where you can have some privacy and create it. Sometimes you may feel you have to create this secure bubble while standing up. If you, for instance, have stress around you, you will want to make sure you feel your feet secured just to the Earth. Head up and feet down. Breathe, find your centre and then feel and create…

PROTECTION – TO SHIELD / EMBRACE ONESELF

What does it mean to protect oneself?
I am not so fond of the word protection. It feels that I assume there are energies that will cause me harm and I am defenceless. I do want to be the one who makes the decision of what density of energies shall pass through me and my "bodies". I do have days where my energy levels are not as vibrant as I wish them to be and I don't feel so strong in handling the "outside" world. I am always very aware of most actions around and within me. I believe that I have my own Body-homeopath inside me. She is always looking for issues to release on my behalf. Say I am working with some anger issues one day and I don't seem to be able to release or find the core of the anger. I know my Body-Homeopath will find a person who will stir up anger in me so I have to react and can be released. When you enter the world of magick, opening up your senses to the "unseen world," the world that is harder to perceive with your naked eye and is mainly sensed or felt, you are bound at the same time to work upon developing your preciseness. This will make you more alert and sensitive to what happens around you. This is completely natural and affects most people. As you raise your vibration within, you get better and better at shielding yourself from what feel to be dense energies. At the same time that you are raising your frequency within, it also requires that you become more and more aware and sensitive. The importance is to establish a foundation supported by Earth. So your body always knows its earthly "home base" and can have a "safe" feeling while in

full contact with your Source. Your balance within will be more stable and it will allow you to take off both within and outside and to dance more freely in between the realms of here and there. Remember that your thoughts and your intentions are always your best friend. What you think and manifest will happen (maybe not instantly). The more focus you have, the faster it will be brought into place. You are bound to place yourself in many situations, and many may seem harder to work through than others. By being aware of all that is happening, you can take action upon the issue and release what is keeping you from moving forward. Let life have its cause. Find your inner strength and dance with ease and flow in your steps.

Meditation / Ceremony

During a meditation or when doing a ceremony, it can be wise to draw a circle around you, or use any other geometric symbol that resonates with you to feel safe. Visualize or draw the form around you. Choose a colour that you feel will support you as well as have your intention clear and strong about what the support shall be about.
Don't be surprised if the symbol might want to rise and surround the whole of you, even if you draw it on the ground.

Out in restaurants or any other public area

If you like to hang out with your friends at restaurants, pubs or go dancing, the energies are more likely to be filled with emotions released by the help of alcohol or drugs. There is bound to be a lot of movement in the etheric field and that can be hard to withstand.
I always create a bubble around me so I am in my own energy vibrations during the evening, and will then be more aware of the party energies around me.
Sometimes I like to have a glass of wine or a beer and then I need to be very in tune with my body. If I get the indication that my body needs 5 glasses of water as an add-on to my one glass of wine, I will drink that or endure the consequences. If you start to sway and feel a little weird, you might suddenly remember that you have forgotten to shield yourself. Seek a quiet corner or preferably walk outside. Take a few deep breaths and empty the energies that you have consumed that are not in resonance with you. Then from the core of your heart exhale a supportive bubble of energy all throughout your bodies.

Responsibility

What is important is that you decide what kind of feelings and vibrations you want to surround yourself with. Do not be ashamed to say no to dance with the energy that emerges from your family and friends, co-workers or someone you like. There is usually not more to it than people don't have the strength to take responsibility for their own emotions, so if there is a chance to give it away, well that is what happens…

Standing in a queue

If you are standing in a queue and you instinctively feel that someone wants to access your energy, locate who that is. Take a few deep breaths to empty the energies that you have consumed that are not in resonance with you, then from the core of your heart exhale a supportive bubble of energy all throughout your bodies.
Always bring your awareness to the situation that just occurred. Why did you let it happen?

Sleeping

We have the ability to leave or expand our body when we sleep and it can happen that your physical body wakes up before the other is in place, this can be very uncomfortable. Breathe as calmly as you can, pray and wait for the bodies to fall into place and then remember to tell your body that this was just a nightmare etc.

The curtain

If you need to have some peace and quiet around you, at work, walking to town on a Saturday, being in the grocery store during rush hour, sitting on the bus.
Pull down an energy curtain around you that allows you to be in your space for the time needed. *Pull up the curtain when it is no longer needed, or you might miss out on something that would bring a smile to your heart.*

MEDITATION TO CREATE GOOD FLOW

Intention is to create a flow of steadiness…

1. Sit down, take some deep breaths and relax with every exhalation, let energy emerge from your heart and surround your whole body, you are safe and in balance.
2. Light the White fire for aiding and transformation.
3. Focus your mind on the day that lies before you (or the situation you wish to focus on)
4. Imagine clear light flowing through the whole day

5. Imagine a rising golden spiral running through and around the day, bringing all the grace and beauty of Creation into this day, making everything smooth, simple and divine.
6. Connect to the energies that you wish for to manifest themselves (joy, love, efficiency, structure, communication) throughout and being embraced by your heart energy, then inhale the energies you have chosen to support you for this task (physical energy, alertness, strength).
7. Let the white fire surround you while you send thanks to the supporting energies, yourself for letting go and your fellow beings for this day.
8. Take a breath, feel your feet placed balanced and steady on the ground
9. When finished, let a breath emerge from your heart feel the bubbling new energy just filling I you up, and let the body create the "space-you-need-for-today".
10. Take tree breathes with the intention to return to Now, move your limbs, open your eyes, smile and just be…

UPGRADE THE ENVIRONMENT YOU ARE SPENDING TIME IN

Once after I had been attending an intense weekend of releasing old patterns within myself, I couldn't wait to get home to rest in my sanctuary, my castle of delight and safety. I tumbled in and just dropped to the floor and wanted to dissolve, as I always do. Instead I had a hard time breathing, I wanted to leave, I felt all but safe. I went outside and I felt fine and as soon as I entered my home, the feelings returned. I was stunned. I didn't know whom to call, I surrounded myself with a heavy cloak of light, made a cup of tea, dressed warmly and placed myself outside and contacted my higher Me and asked for some guidance.

I was shown how I looked before the weekend and then how and where in myself and my bodies the changes had occurred. I saw my energy field around me dancing in shimmering peachy rays. Then I was shown the energy density and how the colours were inside my apartment, how the peachy shimmers just died off and how I got into a defensive frame of mind towards my sanctuary. I was told that I had to upgrade my apartment as well. It had never occurred to me that my home kept that much of my life energy (even if I had worked hard for it to be just so). I upgraded, I connected to the entire weave inside my home and let my heart pour out and asked for us to be merged. When it was done, it was with a fluttering feeling I went back inside, to my favourite spot, laid down and dissolved…… Since then, when I return home, I always make sure I am being merged with my home and that we dance the same moves before I enter. And if you are not living by yourself in your home, be sure that they also are benefiting from the upgrade, preferably tell them about the rise in vibration that will occur. My suggestion is that you think about where you spend a lot of time and merge with these spaces. If it's a space where you are not alone or that does not belong to you, like a work place, you will have to ask the "place" before you merge. This is your journey and maybe your work colleagues are not interested in joining you.

THE ART OF CLEANING

I once a had friend living with me and before her boyfriend arrived, she cleaned our house and made it look beautiful. After he went and the house looked quite shabby I was curious of how long she would take to make it nice for "us". The days went on and I couldn't stand walking in the dirt anymore. I awaited her return and asked her why she had cleaned the house before her boyfriend came for a visit? The answer was what I expected; she wanted to make an impression, wanted to make sure that he felt in comfort etc. My next question was; how come you don't think we deserve the same feeling? And I waited for the "light bulb to go off". When it finally did, she looked at me embarrassed and said, got it! Then I showed her my thoughts behind cleaning. What I would like to point out is that it is what the "eyes" see when entering a house. All your senses are on alert, especially if it's a first time visit...

Think about this

∂   How do you want to be welcomed into your home?
∂   If you are being greeted of a dirty hall mat plus garbage bags when you go for a lunch visit at your friends house, how does this makes you feel, when walking around in the rest of the house? Are you looking for spots on your plate, before pouring the soup you are having for lunch?
∂   When you change your sheets in the bed, do you also think about all thoughts, emotions etc that has been going on there? What would you do to clear them?
∂   What does your workspace reflect about you?

These are my suggestions and thoughts about keeping a house clean

∂   Hallway; clutter free, shoes, clothes etc in order. This is the first impression and will decide your feel for the rest of the house.
∂   Bathroom; clean of course (in all corners) and add that the toilet-seat should be down (would you like to be greeted with my energetic dump?)
∂   Kitchen; clean in all areas, fridge, dishcloth not smelly etc

∂   All seating areas free from dust and crumbles if you are living in a shoe free house make sure the floors are suitable to walk upon in your socks.

∂   Beds; place a white fire under the bed, so all that are released at night, will be transformed

I want my house or work space to feel like it's flexible, that many different personality types can feel at home there. I also want people to respect my space and by showing them energetically and physically how I treat my home, I indicate that that is how I would like them to treat it too.

This goes for my car and all my other belongings too.

HOW TO BALANCE YOURSELF WITH A QUICK AND EASY METHOD

Often we feel in distress. It is hard to keep having a full contact with your body, it feels like the mind and the body are walking on two sides of the street. What I always do is to make sure that I am in contact with the whole of me. That means physical body, your mind worms and your etheric bodies. Without gathering the whole of me, well I can't guarantee that my exercise will be as good as my intention or that it will last for very long. In this exercise I use a crystal to assist me.

1. Sit in comfort, breathe with the intention that shimmering light emerges out from your heart, this light makes connections with all of your bodies and the result is a feeling of peace and clarity in combination with curiosity

2. Breathe and connect yourself with your Higher Self and let yourself expand as much as you can, continuously filling yourself with the shimmering light…

3. Ask your body where the distress you feel is placed. What chakra is involved? If there is more than one, be sharper in your intent and ask which holds the core of the distress, when you are aware of what chakra, body part it is all about, this is how you proceed;

4. Keep your focus and ask your body of the best suggestion to release the distress and to be brought back in total balance.

5. Decide how long your intent to work with this issue will be, then tell your bodies this. If you don't decide the release can go on for a longer time period than wanted.

6. Then say out loud that you want to release the distress from your physical body in harmony and balance, with ease (no strong purges). You can expect changes in your sleep, food intake, skin, that is normally though.

∂   *When you say it out loud, you engage your physical sensory system as well…*

7. Choose a crystal that balances the chakra. Work intuitively, by letting your body and senses choose, or read about what crystal matches your chakra.

8. Place the crystal in a jar of spring water (make sure the glass is without any patterns) at the size that can support you with 10 glasses of water during this week.

∂ Keep the jar during a day and night, preferably under the rays of the Sun or and the Moon. When this is done you are to take a glass of water each day, your choice if the intake is at the morning or bedtime.

∂ Maybe you want to add a little water in a small bottle as a carry-on for daily use if needed.

∂ *If there is still water left you can by adding some alcohol preserve it (50/50) for later use, be sure that you remember what issue made you choose this crystal, it might be the same chakra but not the same issue you would like to encounter another time*

9. Choose an exercise that moves the body part you are working with, there are excellent yoga positions to find and work with. Best is to do the exercise in the morning in combination with making a chakra sound, a mantra song or an AUM.

10. Breathe through and expand the chakra, this is something you can do during the whole day, make sure it is done before you start your morning and before you fall asleep.

11. When the week is over, meditate and scan your body with full awareness in truth towards yourself. Is there anything left? If so, how can you address this?

Tip! This is an excellent way to start communicating with your body, your sensory systems and become more "whole" in the aspect of that all of you are aiming towards being One. You will notice a difference very quickly…

WORDS YOUR BODY MAY VIBRATE IN TUNE WITH

These words can be of support in tracing the root cause of an issue. If you feel overwhelmed, is it possible that you can find any connection to something emotional or physical happening in your life? For example; too much computer work or circling a never ending story about your recent breakup in your mind. You might find or feel that you want to use other words … what's stopping you …

The way I use these words are this; I recognise that I have this "never ending spinning feeling, emotion, words" in my body or mind. I do a body scan/feel and find that the area around the liver is bloated. I have also had a craving for beetroots, which I know from previous times strengthen my liver and this confirms my feeling. I look up the words correlating the liver which are pained and satisfied and with an honest truth towards myself, I admit that I am pained from an old issue that I thought I had worked through.... Then I go into action! I can look up a good crystal that strengthens either the liver or the issue I am holding onto. I will find some physical exercise to do (yoga, meridian stretch etc). I can look up some good flower essences to work with, the list is endless and it is your choice how to address the issue.

Organ	Negative	Positive
Gallbladder	proud	humble
Lungs	depressed	happy
Pineal gland	speechless	communicative
Thymus	anxious	calm
Heart	un-safe	safe
Eye	overwhelmed	successful
Stomach	unpredictable	predictable
Ear	unsupportive	supportive
Salivary gland	grumpy	joy filled
Pituitary gland	disappointed	consolidated
Spleen	cowardly	brave
Bladder	meaningless	hopeful
Pancreas	rejected	admitted
Blood sugar	unaccepted	accepted
Thyroid	humiliated	dignified
Liver	pained	satisfied
Hypothalamus	undesirable	appealing
The skin	worried	harmonious
Small intestine	un-appreciated	appreciated
Large intestine	raging	mild
Reproductive organs	concerned	carefree
Kidneys	shamed	honourable

A good advice someone gave me once; be responsible for your actions and then you have worked out more than 50% of the imbalance...

THE GRID OF LIGHT

Visualize a grid of light, a web that surrounds everything that is alive or made out of live material. The auric field which surrounds an item or a being is different from this. The field acts more like a link between your Source and the light of the living. Each string/thread is not just a line of something. They are pipes that contain infinite light. Sometimes when I am in deep meditation or my senses are heightened I can clearly perceive this grid structure around me. I like to play with it, stretch it, and see how flexible it is. Does it surround more than one item or does it have a connection with more (like a sofa and the chairs and table that belongs together). It somehow soothes me to think that there is a grid that surrounds all of us. There is talk about the "collective", that all belongs and are tied together; well it sure looks like it.

Free your inner Light

This exercise is about freeing light that is stuck for some reason within an item. Be clear of your intention. Do you want to clean, release, open up, make it more inviting, etc.?

It can be that you have bought an old sofa and it seems dense and dirty even if it's clean. By flicking around in the grid that contains the sofa, you will free the energy within and the result will not wait to show itself.

1. Connect your heart energy to the grid. The heart is a more sensitive tool than your third eye and will guide you more gently through the experience.
2. Imagine that you stick your fingers into some of the pipes and that you merge with the whole grid. Start moving your fingers and flick out some sparkling light. See how it starts to spread all around in the grid.
3. Let your fingers relax and fill them with energy from the grid and then start to scatter the light.
4. When you feel and see that the whole grid is sparkling, when you feel that all the pipes are being opened and that the item you have worked on has changed its energy, you are done.

This can be adopted on everything that is alive. Fill your crystals, your plants if they look a little sad, your apartment, etc. If there is any heavy energy within or outside of you, it can all be released with a little splash of sparkling light.

You will now get some more exercises to play around with

Socks

1. Take off your socks.
2. Stand up and feel how the feet and toes are feeling against the floor, notice if and how you are standing. On your toes, back on your heels, toes etc.
3. Sit down in comfort. Take a deep breath, merge your heart light and let it spread throughout your bodies. When you feel at peace, connect your heart energy to one sock and start splashing in light.
4. When it feels like the sock is filled with sparkling lights you put on both socks, stand up and feel the difference between your feet. And then you do the other foot.

A body part

1. Stand up and feel into your legs. Put some focus on your knees. How do they feel?
2. Focus on your right kneecap and begin to scatter the light.
3. How does your knee feel in contrast to the rest of the leg?

An object

1. Hold the object in your hand. Feel its grid. Feel how big its aura has become. You can use a pendulum if you want to measure the size of the aura.
2. Connect your heart energy to the centre of the object and fill up the object with the light from your heart and when you feel connected, start to scatter the light. Create some sparkles out from the grid into the object.
3. When you are done, how does the object feel? Has the aura changed in size, colour, and density?

Person to Person

1. Place yourself opposite the person.
2. Measure how big the chakras radiate forward, backwards and around the person. You can use a pendulum if you want to measure the size.
3. Choose a chakra to balance imagine the grid of light that holds it.
4. Tune in to the chakra with your heart energy, when you feel the connection, start scattering the light.
5. When you feel that you are done, check the chakra. How has the energy from the chakra improved?

REFLECTIONS

Actions!

- ∂ What do you do to be aware of your actions and realize how they affect others?
- ∂ What do you do to understand what energies you send out and how they affect others?
- ∂ Do you carry the ability to communicate, to express what you need?
- ∂ What happens within you if you continuously get misunderstood?
- ∂ Do you carry the awareness of what your aim is?
- ∂ What tools do you carry to break, balance, and release your own old patterns?
- ∂ Where can you seek support?

Healing!

- ∂ What signifies a healer or a person that works with energies for you?
- ∂ What is the primary essence of healing, energy work?
- ∂ Who gets to be healed?
- ∂ Who is healing who?

Safety!

- ∂ Where do you find yourself in total safety?
- ∂ Whom do you seek safety with?
- ∂ Who can seek safety with you?
- ∂ Where in your body is your safety centre?
- ∂ Do you carry too much safety, so there is no room for action?
- ∂ Do you dare to meet the energy of your own safety to see what and how it affects you and your life?

Fear!

- ∂ What is fear?
- ∂ What does your fear consist of?
- ∂ How do you and your body express fear?
- ∂ Where do you hold your fear in your body?
- ∂ Do you want to release it, for good?
- ∂ What can you do to make this happen?

Love!

- ∂   What does it mean to love?
- ∂   Do you fully love all aspects of yourself?
- ∂   What actions do you take when showing love?
- ∂   Where does your love reside in your body?
- ∂   How do you show others that you are in need of love?
- ∂   How do you treat someone that expresses the need of being loved?
- ∂   Is there anything that hinders you to love fully, without conditions, yourself and others?
- ∂   How does it make you feel when you are truly loved by another person, for just being you?
- ∂   Can you carry that feeling on?

Why not create more expressions and answer them, like confidence, silence, grief, joy, interest the list can be as long as you want…

TO PLAY AND EXPLORE WITH A PARTNER

When my conscious energy life started, I had the fortune to attend small and intimate workshops, where we all held curiosity high, expectations were not in our vocabulary, we were just happy and content that we had found people who felt the same, it was all about evolving ourselves. I feel I was very fortunate. There was magic in the air and I loved it.

Our bodies and minds like to be in control over situations. They like to know that they have done well. One way to do this is to train our sensory system (hearing, listening, seeing, touching and feeling). Most of us have one sense, that we feel more confident in and that is the one that we seldom question. Train this one to perfection so you hold no doubts about the "answers" you receive, and then move on to train the other ones thoroughly and with a lot of persistence you will sooner or later find that you are using more of you in situations needed. We usually experience feelings of doubt when we open up to the "unseen" world. Be sure of how you relate to being and feeling doubtful and be in balance with this before you start to challenge yourself. There are many ways to practice. Many require a partner. Ask someone who has an open mind and will enjoy being your practice partner as well as give good constructive feedback.

Remember that your brain loves a good play moment. It will keep it engaged, alert and happy. Good if you keep your faith, have no judgement towards yourself and stay in your body, your Earth energy. Before you start, sit in comfort. Breathe long, deep breaths. When you feel relaxed connect to the core of your heart. Breathe and merge with your entire physical body, continue to breathe and allow yourself to be embraced by your heart energy, connecting to all of your bodies and your Higher Self. Sit in that energy and just be for a moment. When you feel ready, contact and connect yourself with your partners Higher Self and bodies and ask for a blessing to continue with your intent, which is to scan them, to connect with them on a deep level, to interpret their energies…

To pull down the rainbow

Imagine a rainbow above and around you.

1. Connect to each colour until you feel that you are one with the rainbow.
2. Feel and see how each colour comes through your crown, passes through the core of your heart and out through the palms of your hands. You are sending the rainbow through your body.
3. Next step is to connect to your partner and scan the body to see and feel where they need an extra boost of energy. Also ask their body to give you a picture, a word or a sense of what it is lacking and why the colour would support them into being balanced.
4. Then after the colour transmissions are being done, check with the body and ask if it feels content. It is up to you if you want to share the experience with your partner during the practice or after.
5. When you have your picture in mind, start by sending the colour through your hands into your partner's body.

You can place your hands upon them physically and bring them in or just via your thoughts.

Chakra readings with fabrics

A similar practice after the rainbow is to go deeper into the scanning and transmissions.

1. Place your partner sitting in comfort and blindfold their eyes.
2. Place a shawl or a long piece of fabric, preferable in a neutral colour in their hands and ask them to connect themselves, relax into the situation and prepare to open up for the scanning.
3. Blindfold your own eyes.
4. Place yourself opposite your partner and take the other end of the shawl in your hands

5. Connect and start to scan each chakra, start from one end to another (then you don't have to think about what order you worked in) and / or have a third person available with pen and paper who can takes notes.

Whatever you see, sense, perceive you tell out loud. When the interpretation is done, you connect to the rainbow within you and send colours to balance the chakras.

Drawing the auric fields

1. Have a big paper and colour pencils ready. Draw a body.
2. Place your partner in front of you, preferably standing up.
3. Connect and ask the body to show you what colours it has around itself and start to paint the colours.

There are no rules. The aura shifts in colours and motions as quick as a thought passes through. Just enjoy perceiving the palette of colours coming through to you
Don't be surprised if you are being shown symbols, pictures and maybe even tunes of music. Let it all come through you and remember it might not make sense for you, but when you start to explain and show the person what you have drawn, it will make sense to them.

The mirror

1
∂ Look in your own eyes in a mirror
∂ How does it feel?
∂ What do you see?
∂ What do you perceive?

2.
∂ Look into your partner's eyes and perceive.

To share spinal energy

1. Place yourself and your partner back-to-back. Sit in comfort.
2. Start breathing and when you feel that your breaths are in sync with each other as well as sharing that intimate space, you start to connect your spinal energy with each other

3. Inhale and push the breath up through the spine, you are now sharing and have only one spine

4. Exhale and move the breath down. Continue until you are in total sync and balanced, then expand the spine so it embraces both of your bodies, you are now sitting inside a tube of pure light force

5. Turn around and face each other, without losing the feel of that you have this great connection

6. Look into each other's eyes and start to feel, see, perceive, and meet each other

7. The first task is to locate and perceive your partners inner child, ask the child to connect and if it has a message that it wants you to give

8. Secondly you connect to your inner child and ask if it's anything that you should understand and know

9. When you are done, sit with the feeling for a while and then start to separate yourself from each other

10. Return back into your own spinal energy, your own body, your own senses

11. Anchor yourself through your heart. Open your eyes and allow yourselves some time to re-connect, but this time in your own energy. Share your experience

YOU ARE MY BELOVED

This is a wonderful exercise that I learned attending a workshop. You need to be at least two persons to perform or you can use a mirror and give yourself a little boost of Love.

Take a breath, centre in your heart and let that energy and feeling merge throughout and surround your bodies. Place yourself in front of your partner and connect with each other by holding hands and breathing together. When your breaths are in sync, look into each other's eyes and start to sing or say at the same time;

∂   "You are my beloved,
∂   I open my heart to you."

Stand in front of each other and look each other in the eyes.
Gently place your hands on each other's hearts.
Hold the intention to reach out to the other person's heart.

∂   Sing "You are my beloved

∂ I open my heart to you" at least 4 times.

Then direct the light emerging from your hearts to each other's energy centres and subtle bodies… It is only your fantasy that stops you from evolving this wonderful heart song and bringing you to places unknown…

When done, connect your breaths once again. Look into each other's eyes and when you both feel in sync, embrace each other. If there are several people, switch partners and repeat the exercise until you have connected with everyone from the heart space.

Tip: This is a very strong exercise and can be very emotional. Please care for each other…

CHAPTER 3

TOOLS

THE TOOLS

Healing tools! Do you need them? Is it necessary to make them by myself or shall I be given the tools? What shall I buy, can I trust the people who are making them, or do I need a special person to create them?

I remember in the beginning of my path I felt bombarded by all these questions that came up for me are. Should I use tools, what if I make a mistake and just make a fool out of myself? What if my clients ask me about the tools, and they know more than me. Wow!

Sometimes I believe that we shall just be. We know, we walk down memory lane and I am sure that we will find that we have all the tools, or have had at some time. In my last cleanse in the attic, I found little bells, maracas, a shell and a lot of nice strings, new tools! A tool for me is something that I can use to enhance a treatment, a ceremony or a meditation. It makes it more focused and helps me to hold space or clear it. After a session I like to collect the auric field of the person and connect it to the physical body again, and depending how the constitution of the person is, I will use a feather, a bell, a pendulum or a rainstick, sometimes I tune and sing some mantras or just a simple amen or aum. I love beautiful things, I am also very efficient, so I guess the tools I use are a mix of them both. I once visited an intuitive for a reading and suddenly she said "now I know" and she left and returned with an item in a plastic bag. She handed me the bag and said, don't look, just feel...hrmm...feel, what for, what's in the bag, imagine all these questions that raced through my mind, I mean I was there to have a chat with my dead granny...anyway, I felt and I was struck by lightning and I peak into the bag and saw a blue stick. I asked her again and she said "with time, you will find out". That was that. I can tell you that I brought my stick to many and asked them what it was, and it was only one person, who actually understood the sincerity I was in and she tried to tune in and help out. I can say that I still use it after nearly 25 years, it's a super grounding tool for my clients and I usually don't show them until after what I placed upon them. It has got 3 faces with hanging tongues and it's a little scary J. Your tool, your magickal item is something you charged for a special purpose. With the intent of bringing in calmness to your house, you might have flowers in colours that make you relax. You might have scented candles for the ambience, but charged with the intent to open up for Magick, and the list goes on. I will present some items that are magical for me, which I use

Voice

∂ Your own voice is a powerful tool. You do not have to be a singer to be able to use your vocal cords to tune and clear energies.

Breath

∂ To use your breath to disperse stagnant energy in the auric field by blowing where it feels stuck.

Hands

∂ Use your hands to work just upon the body with a feathered touch and then let your hands work intuitively around and in the auric field. Do not work too fast in the aura. The movement can create waves that make the person nauseated, although some who experience a "wave" in the aura can sometimes feel like they are flying, and find it is wonderful.

Feather

∂ A feather is a fantastic tool to use in and around the auric field, to mend, to open up, to close and to disperse energy.

Rattle

∂ Rattle is also a tool you may find useful. If you find something really stuck in the body or in the aura, use your rattle and shake it loose.

Stick

∂ A stick that you attach beautiful stones upon, examples in the colours of the rainbow, wrapped with copper wire, can be used as an "extended" arm to draw symbols over your energy depots to give an extra "boost" of energy.

Stones

∂ Stones found in nature, why not choose all four elements, loaded in the energy of the sun or the moon, painted with a special symbol, these can be added as an extra support placed upon the body during a session or simply put a stone in their hands.

Essences

∂ Flower and Stone Essences that you either buy or create yourself are wonderful to use both before and after a session, meditation or in any creative process.

Incense

∂ I love using this as a tool, to cleanse the aura.
  When I want to say thank you to Earth, in a ceremony or an offering, I light incense

Bags

∂ Make your own or buy a beautiful and functional bag to keep all your tools in, where you can carry and bring everything you need.

It is only your own imagination that can possibly limit you in creating a tool with a specific intent. Everything can be used. Go searching within and outside yourself, tune in and start to play…

TO DANCE WITH THE STONE PEOPLE

I have a love affair with stones. Since childhood I have collected, shared my inner most secrets, cried, loved and embraced my Stone people. I used to collect special stones for special occasions. As a child I had a tummy stone, since whenever there were big family gatherings, I seemed to be in cramps after dinner and my stone always supported me in transforming the energies I had consumed. I scraped off the glitter that I found on the stones by our lake, and the shimmer made me so happy. The first time I entered a crystal exhibition, I was very close to fainting, and my body exploded in so much happiness. I was in there for hours and the owner just smiled and made no attempt to push me into buying anything, as he saw and appreciated what went on with me. I wish I could have thanked him then, but being in a daze I just went home and crashed. My suggestion to you is that you find your own dance with the Stone people. For me they hold the key to a lot of things, because they have been here for so long and they have an inner knowing. You can connect yourself to the stone and receive your story, because it is held there and it will be shared when the time is ripe. I do not always follow what stones I need for specific occasions by reading about them beforehand. I simply tune in and ask which stone would be willing to support me in my task. Afterwards I may sometimes get curious and I will look up the properties of the stone to receive a deeper understanding.

There are many power places around the world – and we have many in Sweden – which are said to be burial grounds since thousands of years back. I have come upon many and they sometimes feel like they are a little dense or dormant and some people get a feeling that they do not want human contact. Well I know that the Stone people like to get embraced so I look at this differently. A power place is unfortunately a place where we humans tend to go and take power away, and we usually leave some sort of gift, but it might not be the gift that balances what we received, which means we deplete the energy. I suggest that you open your heart fully and approach the Stone people bringing just yourself and wait for their response. Then you can merge. I had a question once when I was about to conquer my first mountain peak (I have slight vertigo) and as I stood there on my way up and suffering from vertigo with the path being wet, slippery and steep and wondering how I would make it, a voice came and asked, "What do you want from me?" "Nothing," I said honestly, I just want to overcome my fears and pat myself on my shoulder for making it across my first peak. Right then I was showered in a soft light and I knew someone, for me it was the mountain spirit, was supporting me up that peak. Enough about me. Now I will suggest some easy steps on how to work with the Stone people.

Having Stone people to support you in your goals is adding some depth and power to your task. They will hold space for you, as in that the energy coming from the Stone people will assure that you can work in peace. They will act similar to guards during the time required, and they can be programmed for various tasks and help you keep your mind more focused while holding them. In other words, they have an endless repertoire, so start to communicate and just merge with them. To explain what you actually do, you access the energy structure in the crystal and give it a task. You alter the structure so the stone can receive instructions, like you give a command to a computer, although they wouldn't quite agree as they are alive and a computer is not.

There are two ways to encode stones. Either use / program a specific stone for just one thing, so it gets used to working with "what is" e.g. you have your special dream-stone that is used as such. This is called this single-handed encoding. The other way is that with a clear, focused intention decide what the stone will be used for and encode it with that. This is called multi-tasked encoding. Whatever method you choose you have to tune in to the stone and make sure that it can dance in harmony and hold the vibration of the realm you will work in. I have had big crystals that have been broken in two during a session. Oops...

To start your dance with the Stone people

Is getting to know your stone, tune in with it, open your heart from your inner core and feel its vibration. Ask what it can support you with. Some stones might from their beginning have a set task they are set to do and maybe it does not correlate with your desires.
Crystals are considered the mineral kingdom's most perfect and natural creation. Crystals are formed in the womb of Earth, through complex chemical processes that take thousands of years. Quartz is the most abundant crystal on Earth. It is composed of silicon and oxygen, two very common elements in our world. The family of quartz includes rock crystal, amethyst, citrine, smoky quartz and rose quartz. Clear quartz is the most often mentioned in connection with healing and meditation. Crystals have a perfect molecular structure which means that they are always in a state of equilibrium and harmony. A crystal always vibrates with the same frequency. It returns as much energy as it receives. Science has discovered this property of primarily quartz crystal and it is used today in a wide range of technological devices that require precision. Crystals have been shown to affect us humans because of the fact that our bodies are surrounded by an energy field. When you come in contact with crystal, your energy field starts to dance on the same vibration as the crystal and this dance continues until your bodies have reached the same level of vibration as the crystal itself and are in balance.

The crystal can accelerate the healing process, strengthen your nervous system and help to focus your mind by activating your intuition. It also protects your aura and can help awaken dormant healing powers. Crystals also have an inhibitory affect on radiation and radioactivity. A rose quartz on your computer is said to help disperse some activity. Crystal water seems to have a positive effect and enhances the life force in all that is alive. Gemstones have always exercised a great attraction for us humans. We have always used the stones as talismans, jewellery and for their healing abilities. In many ancient cultures, you placed jewellery in tombs, convinced that its magical powers would also appear and support the afterlife. The stones all have their own unique abilities, relating to your bodies, your mind and your overall well-being. During crystal therapy, you can use a variety of crystals and stones. They can be placed around the body in various patterns. If desired, when you choose "your" crystal let intuition guide. Your source always knows which crystal you need at that time.

I have several times in my sleep, created wonderful crystal grids around friends that has slept over, imagine their facial expression when woke up realizing that they have been under the influence all night long.

You can also "self-treat" with crystals. Wear them as jewellery, carry them in your pocket, bra or panties if you are working on any specific issue. I have had several clients who when they undressed had their stones fall out of their clothing and shatter all over the floor. They seemed to forget that they had them on.

Once I managed to over activate myself with crystals and developed an allergy. I was told that I slept above an energy grid so I placed my mattress on top of metal foil to protect myself, not thinking that I had my Stone "moment" at the same time, meaning that I had a bunch of stones under my pillow and around me when I slept. The combination of grid lines, metal foil and all the stones, well it was not the best. I got over stimulated and become extremely sensitive. I took away the foil, found a good Granite stone that supported me with the grids and then had one crystal under my pillow instead.

Encoding the stones

1. Tune into the crystal, so you can be in tune with its energy and ask for permission to start the dance.
2. Wait for the response. If you don't feel in complete harmony choose a different stone.
3. Ask the stone to open up its source of wisdom and power so it can receive your programming and hold the space needed. Wait until you feel that there is an open flow and the stone is open to receive.
∂ If the stone was to be used for a single-handed encoding (like a dream stone) you say your thanks and place it in its special place until used.
∂ For a multi-task encoding, be sure of your intention. I suggest you write down exactly what kind of support you seek from it.

∂ It is important that the vibration coming from you and the purpose is in harmony with the stone, so you will have a good partnership.

1. Sit in comfort, breathe and connect to your inner heart. Let that energy merge with the rest of your bodies until you feel that you are One with your source.
2. Allow your mind and stone to meet on an energy plane, so they get to know each other better. Wait for a feeling of acceptance from the stone until you let your mind flow into the stone. Focus your awareness on the purpose and allow it to merge.
3. Let your heart, your third eye and your body dance with the Stone people and continue the dance until you feel that the encoding is complete
4. Tune into the stone to be sure that the stone feels good, that the encoding is in tune with themstone and your own intention.
5. Visualize that you leave the new encoding in a protective care of the stone and that All is in harmony.

It is said that if you have a quartz crystal with four sides the stone can hold four different codes. Every time you are using the stone, tune into it so it is in harmony and the coding still has the vibration you need. Give it some love and thanks. A double pointed clear quartz crystal is good to use if you want to send and receive energy at the same time. A crystal ball can be used to look into. A laser wand, a one-pointed clear quartz crystal can be used to clear energy fields. But it must be treated with care so there won't be any "burns" in the fields of the etheric bodies.

Crystal Waters are a good way to get access to the crystal's power.

The water usually plays a vital role in making and using the essences. It is said that the energy of the water makes an imprint into the liquid. Everything seems to reflect off, in-to the water. That's why it's important when making essences that the bowl is clean of patterns, so that this does not reflect in the essence that is extracted. Off course you might have a jar with a certain geometric pattern on it. Then this pattern will be infused with the crystal. If you want to cure your nausea, I suggest you don't use a jar replace it with waves unless you find that these waves will support you to find balance. Then you should have that in your intention when coding the water. If you have a fear of the sea and you are on your way to have a sailing vacation, it can be a good idea to pick a stone from the bottom of the sea, tune into it and ask for support and understanding of your discomfort.

Way to go

1. Put your crystal in pure spring water in a clear, pattern-free pitcher for one Sunny day or a Moony night. Ask your stone and body if you benefit from Sun or Moon rays. You can also let the cup be exposed to the rays of the sun or moon.

∂ If you want to work with remembering your dreams better, find a Moonstone and let it dance with the rays of the Mother Moon…

   You can benefit from drinking crystal water every day, I had an "ethereal" iron deficiency and steeped a hematite in my water bottle and drank it until I felt that the balance was restored in my body.

∂ Do you have pms, love troubles, stress, etc? Ask what stone you need and drink the water in the way that correlates at the moment.

   Many drink the water for 21 days if there is a "chronic" issue to balance.

A LITTLE HISTORY ABOUT FLOWER ESSENCES

My initiation with these wonder-filled devas started in my living room. A friend of mine was creating flower essences. She had 72 different ones that she had made herself, but she had only had time to write about a few. I gave a suggestion that I could write a book about them all and we did an exchange of work.

So here I am on my living room floor with 72 bottles and a vibrating energy that jumped around them. I had decided that I should categorize them in elements, chakras and directions as well as a little text about their properties. I had been collecting information from old Swedish books in folk medicine. I found some books about essences, but they were mostly connected to the brand name and vibrated in a different energy than these ones. So with the help of my source, my intuition, I started. Ha! You try to have 72 "little people" wanting your attention, arguing about whether they were a wind or a fire element, what chakras they belonged to, etc. My neighbour came by and wondered with whom I was arguing. Oops. She left more convinced than ever that I was a little "strange". We did it. We managed to all merge in harmony and balance and the book was written. Afterwards I found some books where they mentioned some of my flowers and we had received the same message. Phew. It is one of my most fun memories working with energies and nature devas. I hold them very close to my heart.

The history

It said that for about 40,000 years, the indigenous in Australia have used flowers as part of their natural healing system. In other parts of the world where folk medicine is still alive, the tradition to use flowers is something that has continued through the centuries until today. Many of us instinctively turn to flowers to feel better. It is common to bring flowers to someone to make them happy or show appreciation. It has been believed that the morning dew on a flower carries the essence of the flower and can be scraped off each flower leaf. In Europe Dr. Edward Bach was the one that re-discovered the healing energy powers of flowers and made it popular. He noticed that flowers that caught the sunlight were more charitable in their energy than when they were in the shade. He also discovered that when flowers were floating in a bowl of pure spring water, it gave additional strength to the tincture. The method he created to make flower essences for healing purposes is still in use today with some variations.

Water holds memories

The water plays a vital role in making and using the essences. It seems to have the ability to retain energy. The energy from the flower will create an imprint in the water, and the quality of this vibration is what dances with you when you use them. Do not expect to find any dissolved chemical substances from the flower in the water. All the water contains is the energy. That's why it's so important when making essences that the bowl is clean of patterns so the energy can flow freely while the essence is being created. If you were to create an essence in a bowl filled with spirals, the end product would hold the energy of the flower as well as the spirals. It almost seems unlikely that energized water alone can keep such healing powers in itself. However, there is evidence of this. A French immune biologist named Dr. Jacques Benveniste found that certain substances in very diluted form can be just as effective as much larger quantities of the same substance. I read that in one of his experiments he diluted an allergen so it was no longer "visible" in the water, but it still created an allergic reaction. Somehow water had retained memory or vibration of the allergen molecule and had multiplied itself.

Like everything else living we humans are also filled with energy. This permeates every part of our body and mind and its abundance goes hand in hand with our health and vitality. Life energy flows freely in a newborn baby, but as we continue our journey through life we begin to subdue our energy for different reasons. One way to restore our energy balance is by using flower essences.

Flower essences are unique in their ability to revitalize and "enchant" us. We experience an overall feeling of well-being throughout our body and mind, and they act as the perfect antidote to the stress we are exposed to. Fatigue is a sure sign that our body's energy balance is in flux. We might take a vacation to recharge the batteries, but it is rare to have time to trace the fatigue back to its origin. The beauty of flower essences is that they have the power to bring our system back into balance. Flower essences will act as a catalyst for the body's vital energy. They bring us back to our original balance so that we can reach perfection in our genetic blueprint. They vibrate very much like our own energies and get to the areas of the body that need the most attention. Flower essences are taken up directly by the blood and within minutes end up in our meridian system, which forms an energetic interface between the "higher body" and the physical body.

Essences can be used several ways

Flower essence is vibrating energy. The best way to become aware of their effects is to surround yourself with them, both inside and outside.

Mouth

The traditional way to take essences are to put a few drops under the tongue for a minute. Placing them right there seems to be the quickest way to get them into the meridian, our energy system. The method is described as coming from the time, when ancient healers drank dew from flowers to capture their valuable properties. Dew was seen by many ancient people as a mysterious substance appearing magically out of the vastness of the night sky: first absent and then suddenly there, as if produced by nature's metamorphosis from dark to light. This form of water, with all of its life-giving powers silently and subtly appearing out of the night, was viewed as mysterious and full of auspicious qualities. Avoid contact between the dropper and tongue. If you touch it, bacteria can easily begin to grow in the bottle. The essence can also be dropped in liquids like water, juice, herbal tea, if for some reason you can't take it directly in the mouth. Avoid use in regular coffee or tea though. You can dilute the essence quite a lot. The result is it will work on more subtle levels.

The skin

Essences work well when added to your skin. Good places to apply them would be the top of the head, forehead, lips, ankles, soles and palms. This method is good when someone cannot take the essence by mouth. You can also drop them in creams, oils and use them during a massage treatment, preferably in the hands of the therapist.

The bath

To take a bath - 30 minutes - and add some relaxing essence in the bath is a nice way to get some extra relaxation. If you want to get the maximum benefit you can put pure sea salt in the bath when it is being filled up.

Body Spray

To spray your body with essences (blended in spring water) is a very effective way to treat sensitive skin, eczema, ulcers, etc. Put seven drops in a bowl of spring water, and if possible have it in the sun for a day, which add some extra energy to the spray. Spray the part of the body that needs attention and just let it dry. In acute cases of insect bites, wounds, and shock, you can spray several times a day. Another way to make use of the essences is to spray your pillow if you have difficulty falling asleep.

Room Spray

Spraying essences in the air is a great way to clean a room. Drip 4-5 drops in a 250 ml bottle filled with spring water and spray when needed. You can benefit from using this method, when you are sick with flu, have allergies or suffer with respiratory issues. To use an essence that enhances your immune system, like when people around you have winter colds, is a good idea. They can also calm a stressed environment.

How to make your own essences

It is basically very simple. With humbleness, intuition and sunlight you will do great.

1. Use a completely un-patterned glass bowl. This is important. It should preferably be used only to make flower essences. Also you have to rinse it thoroughly each time it is used.
2. Add clean and fresh spring water without contaminants and chlorine, heavy metals or otherwise. Do not put your fingers in the water or poke at the inside of the bowl. It is best to use tools as wood or glass. It is all about the vibration.
3. Time to go out in nature and select a flower that is willing to share its powers and become an essence.

∂   When you find the flower you seek, always tune in and ask for assistance. Use your intuition or another tool that you use for these purposes. It is very important that everything is in perfect balance. Flower, location, time, the bowl, the weather and especially the harmony should flow in total balance.

4. When everything is perfect, place the bowl next to the flower and bend it gently into the water.

∂   Do not in any way harm or force the plant. Some break the flowers of the stem and place in the bowl. *I prefer to collect an energy that is alive for my essences.*

∂   Keep the bowl in bright sunlight for about four hours. After these hours, make sure that the water has not been contaminated by any debris, bird droppings or anything else.

∂   If it looks good bring out the little test tool if you have one. Otherwise use your intuition to make sure that you have a strong floral essence concentrated in the bowl.

5. Pour the essence in a glass bottle or jar without contaminating it with your fingers or other items. A glass funnel can be a great help. The concentrate must not come in contact with plastic or metal.

6. In order to concentrate the essence you mix it with alcohol at least 20-40% strong. Most flowers require 20%. Others that have a high frequency like lotus and sunflower require 40% to keep their vibration.

Now you have created your Mother tincture.

7. Then take a small glass bottle (30 ml) with a dropper and drop in 7 drops of the Mother tincture and fill the rest of the bottle up with alcohol, preferably cognac or brandy, you have now created a Daughter tincture. Out of this you drop 3 drops in a 10 ml bottle, fill it with 50/50 spring water and brandy.

8. Shake the bottle with the intention to disperse the energy, keep on until it feels that the bottle vibrates. You have now created your work tool: the baby tincture.

You can use apple cider vinegar, vegetable glycerine, and honey to preserve essences as well. I do however recommend you to use the alcohol when you create the Mother and Daughter tincture to be ensured that you have them preserved. It seems to hold longer.

ELEMENTS

I am choosing to talk about four elements, in other traditions there are five in number. My fifth element would be my Spirit. What do the elements represent for me? Becoming One with nature and calling upon my wild side is the answer to that question. I have since childhood danced with the elements or they have danced with me. Sometimes I am not sure who dances and triggers whom. I am a very emotional person and when it hasn't been okay to release these emotions in public, I have turned towards the elements for support. I do believe that I unwittingly called upon storms to help me dissolve the motion within. There have been times when I have tried to challenge the elements. Once I had a profound healing experience and my whole Me was in turmoil. It was raining and I went outside to merge with the elements. Cursing the weather and the turmoil that didn't release itself inside from within me, I challenged the wind. I said that I would make it stop with my fierce emotion from within and then "they" had to help me with my raging emotions. I was standing in the wind and the rain, refusing to let go of my emotions and just when I felt the wind slow down a little a thought went through my mind, Ha! I won….

Or not…I am not kidding when I say that the Wind can actually laugh, that was what it was doing when it lifted me off my feet and landed me on my bottom very muddy and very wet laughing at myself and my stupidity. I said out loud, "Okay, you won. I give up, I release my emotions," and it all went quiet…

After that lesson from my Mother Earth, I wanted to learn how to integrate with the elements instead. I have patiently learned how to listen, perceive and merge with them. I love them dearly, I have memories of merging with them at a young age and I have found my way back to that playfulness that taught me to dance with them without fear but with a great respect.

In my country Sweden we have a saying that the stones are trolls that have been put to sleep and they are hard to wake up. They are guardians. They hold wisdom and they are not easy to flirt with. I think I have found a way though. I just place my whole Me upon them and let them be curious about me instead of the other way around.

It is said that that Fire and Air / Wind represent the male aspect, as being more active. Water and Earth represent the female aspect being more passive. I believe that all elements have an active and a passive side to them. The fire when it's in full blast is active, strong, hot and alive, keeping your senses alert. When the fire turns into ashes, there is still heat but the energy is more subdued and calms your senses. Water can trickle and be like gentle kisses upon your face as well as the creek becoming a roaring river with a strong current that sweeps all with her. The wind can turn from a nice breeze into a tornado, moving houses around. The Earth can open herself up easily when it is time to plant the seeds as well as swallow a whole village in a quake. During a week I got an assignment from my Source regarding the elements and that I had to connect with them and try to figure out what they were all about, this is what I received.

Wind

By breathing in my intention, I automatically enhance the source of truth in my body, and the connection with the outer and inner world has reached a completion within.

One of the best ways to cleanse out negative energy from the lungs and lymphatic system is Fire breathing for me, holding the intention to expand from the source within throughout all layers of my being. (Negative energy is all that holds a denser and lower vibration than I hold.)

Water

My body carries the knowledge of how to cleanse itself. It is about cleansing my auric field and the depths of how far I can reach inwards, towards my chakras and the flow of the fascia and meridians, and trusting that they know how deep a cleansing my body can handle

Fire

This is the transformer. Used with skill and intent, this element is the fastest to use when a transformation is needed. There are different colours of this element. I need to find the colour that I resonate with, it depends on what level my physical body vibrates in and the density of the task ahead.

Earth

How transparent can I allow my body to become going deep into the element of Earth?

The density of Earth is an illusion, set up as a protective shield towards intruders. The Earth element makes you carry the element of life within you, so it is my own intent that decides what level of life energy I will work in, where lies my strength? On what levels are my body and senses being prepared to hold this force of life?

HOW TO INTEGRATE THE ELEMENTS

Water

Open your heart, connect to the Spirit of the water and sit down, let the elementals start dancing with you, feel you, play with you, challenge you while you sink in deeper and with more trust for every breath you take, allowing your body finally to become water, moving over the stones, let the current swirl you around and around ….

Earth

Place yourself upon your favourite Earth piece. Open your heart and ask her to bring you inside of her. Feel how your body dissolves in the mass and becomes like air. Feel the density of your body and release the fear of being nothing but a fragment of spirit dancing inside. (I love this one!)

Fire

Breathe and connect your heart with the fire. Ask what you
can do to reach within and anchor in it. Ask the fire to teach you how to transform within it. Sit and connect with the whole life span of the fire, from the blasting energetic part to the ashes. Where is your power held in the element of fire?

Wind Reach out with your heart towards the wind. Let it lift you and help you fly You, let it swirl around within and outside your bodies. Let your auric field be rinsed by the different segments and allow yourself to fly off. There is so much information about the elements to find. I have given you my viewpoints and hope it has inspired you to find your own connection to these wonderful powers.

THE (MEDICINE) WHEEL OF TRANSFORMATION

There are different ways to work in a wheel as is the case in everything we work with.
The purpose of a medicine wheel is to be able to move freely through all of our human experiences, and not get caught in any part. If we want to solve an imbalance, this can be one technique to use. Some traditions start in the direction of East and end in the North and some start in the South and end in the East. What combines them is that they use animals, elements and symbols to charge the wheel. I will give you my interpretation of the wheel. It might not be fully as you have learned or read in a book. But it works for me and holds the power I have needed when it's been activated.

I feel very humble and so happy that I am able to connect to the wise animals and women and men. I believe that they have always walked beside me this lifetime. I have for several reasons not been able to embody them all until now. Being able to let go and let myself open up for an animal spirit fully, that is a wow. Yes, I have to say wow. It is a true delight. Since childhood I have always had a black panther with me. She has been my cuddle, she has been my protector, and she has been with me walking between life and death. I have seen her as a prolonged part of me. Living in Peru and being able to just be and look upon myself differently than before, I started to feel her differently. She came to life, no wonder moving from Sweden to home (as in South America being more of a panthers home than Sweden). I felt that I had to grow up if I wanted to resume my connection with her. One day I woke up knowing that I would go for a ride with her. A little cocky but yet respectful I went into my state of mind and merged with her. I turned into a "twin panther," feeling like a teenager I was eager to "go." She turned her head and looked at me, deeply and said "I eat meat", yeah, yeah, I know, was my reply…no you don't understand I AM A MEAT EATER, and then it hit me: Panthers are hunters. They hunt for meat (and I have not eaten red meat for over 30 years) Oops…in Sweden we have a saying, that if you want to play the game, you better be prepared for what might come upon you. I hunted, we ran, we waited for our prey and I had to attack and kill it. I didn't have to eat it. It was enough to taste warm blood in my system and somewhere the 98% vegetarian in me was in shock. I passed the grownup test, I was accepted and was brought to meet many of my "cat family," and I felt truly at home…

South – the direction of my past

Starting in the South we work through past emotions that no longer serve us, as well as ancestral energies and our own past. The Snake as a symbol of transformation will support you through this. I have many times had the Turtle as support as well. Imagine that the past is a cave and the Snake will guard the entrance so you will be sure of being by yourself in there. Sometimes I have found it a little uncomfortable to look at my past and being on the back of The Turtle when she brings me in the cave has been of great comfort. I can view and perceive what might be in there that I have forgotten to work through or just don't know about. So either sit upon the shell of the Turtle or ask if she can walk beside you during the "walk" down your past. Be open and let the South energies support you walking towards action in your life.

West – the direction of my dreams

Moving on to the West. I love West. Having grown up off the west coast of Sweden I have indulged myself in numerous Sun sets and released my day into the night, knowing that tomorrow will bring in new to my life. For me this is the direction of the Cat people. The Jaguar, the Panther, the Puma, the Lynx, all of them are strong protectors. The Puma in the Andean tradition is the keeper of the middle world, Earth. The Panther and Jaguar are night animals and have no fear of looking and supporting me whilst leaving the old behind. I am moving toward my dreams, letting my visions be united into the Heart weave of my true Spirit.

I have my family of "women" here. My Native American ancestors sing to me and show me how to weave and be true to myself and make me understand what I have chosen to carry with me from them, from my Me into this lifetime…

North – the direction of my wisdom

Moving towards the North brings me into my wisdom and my source of knowledge that I have carried with me to this life. I connect to the Owl, that makes me look at life from all angles and the Hummingbird that makes sure I am seeping the working energies into my heart for support. I have had a need to create a solid foundation that can hold me during the strong and intense transitions bringing back the "old Me," merging her and making her comfortable to live in a more modern body and mind than she is used to. I believe that I am bringing back parts of me in an original form, my star-seed, my first creation, there are many words for this. I am sure you have one, too.

For me the North gate is connected to my mind, my mental part of my body. Calling in the energies from the North means that I am upgrading and merging my old mind. I believe that this old part of me has been kept secured and holds information and wisdom that has been dormant until I was ready to embrace that wisdom and integrate it into my daily life. My grandmother in this life, her second name was Owl, so calling the Owl in feels very secure for me. I know that she will care for me.

East – the directions of my home

Lovely East, where the Sun rises and new beginnings are singing in my heart, supported by the birds, the Eagle and the Condor. Mighty birds that can carry our full etheric weight and take us on a glide in the sky. They give me perspective on my life and any particular situation I am looking upon. I also have a strong connection to the female energy of the White Buffalo. Having her holding space on Earth for me, whilst flying high above is a treat I truly treasure. Returning to the East is like returning home after a long journey, knowing that I am home and secure, and have done the best I could: creating my visions from my heart space and keeping them vivid enough to spill them over and create a solid foundation of faith, trust and joy.

Adding the elements into the wheel

Sometimes I feel I want to add the elements into the directions too.

I choose fire in the East, since the sun is rising. Water in the South since water, when I am in it, feels so transformative. My body yearns for the touch of water when I am doing deep work and this element resonates with the symbol of the Snake, since she is shedding and transforms all the time. West is my earth. The earth is fertile and weaving my creation. I know that I will have the Earth as a "fertilizer" and a strong support for my foundation. The Wind is my north, which blows, releasing and clearing all my old wisdom and bringing the new forth to me.

Explore the wheel of transformation

This is one way you can work with the wheel of transformation. Place yourself in all the directions with your intention. You can choose if you want to place yourself in one direction at the time or expand and embrace them all. It can be a hearty gesture to direct yourself and invoke them separately first and then embrace them. Ask for support so you will receive the information that arises from your heart space, as well as holding a feeling of being secure and gently pushed forward through the wheel of transformation. Sometimes I have worked the wheel backwards, to trace what started a particular action that didn't quite get me where I aimed. For example say you have difficulties with being patient, and then it can be a good idea to go back "in time" in body/mind to seek the root cause of this issue. You will then address your questions differently when directing the directions and when you have received the information you seek, move forward in the wheel with a more intact feeling within. Place yourself in each direction; let your heart reach out to the spirits and the elements in each direction. Feel it, be it, and create your own wheel of transformation.

I very often ask my body to choose a direction, she seems to know and holds a deeper sense than me (especially if it's an old issue I want to release). I have received words, thoughts about the "old way" of merging with these directions and how the "new ways" are moving into my life. Maybe this way of looking at situations and actions will appeal to you too.

East to West

Old:

∂ You have a vision, something you want to accomplish and you are moving the thought, energy of this vision into hoping that it will happen sometime in your future, "a dream" coming through.

New:

∂ You have a vision and with your heart the vision is being weaved into reality.

North to South

Old:

∂ You have a vision and that requires achievement, where you will be judged or compared with others or previous achievements.

New:

∂ You walk with Clarity in mind and your heart towards action. Action does not have to be in physical form. It can be a thought or a statement. It does not involve any competitive energy and doesn't have to involve any other persons.

CAST A CIRCLE

To know if the circle is a symbol you and your bodies resonate with, meditate, connect and breathe with it. Ask to be shown how you can benefit from each other and feel it.

A circle is a lovely symbol to work with.
It unites.
It shields.
It carries a variety of density.
It expands and breathes on its own, keeping the ability to expand and contract.
And it can be turned into a round ball.
As with everything that has to do with energies, be sure of your intent before you start.

∂ If you feel that you need to be in solitude, cast a circle around you to give you some peace and quiet from outer attention.
∂ If you are doing a ceremony and you want all of the participants to be united in one energy flow, cast a circle around you with the appropriate intent (you don't want anyone to feel trapped).
∂ If you walk home at night and feel uncomfortable, ask your heart to create a circle, a ball around you, so you are walking securely in your own energy.

As you know there are many symbols that carry energies that can be suitable in your work. Connect with the ones that attract you and ask.

PENDANT OR PENDULUM

Open your mind and your heart for the opportunities to rise within you. A pendulum will become what you need and want it to be. It can work as your elongated Higher Self," the part of you that knows a little more about yourself. It's the part that may extend your consciousness a bit higher in your everyday life and give you answers to questions that may seem out of reach. You can make use of the pendulum when you want to clear stagnant energies in a room. Stagnant means that the frequencies are not resonating with you or the task you have in mind. Usually they feel too dense. This can be used in your room in your work place, after a party in your home, cleaning up after a workshop or before a meeting in a conference room. The variation only ends were your imagination ends.

Making use of a pendulum is an easy way to start playing and working with energy.

A good start is to let all thoughts be cleared from your mind, breathe through your body until you feel that you are in a balanced space with the whole of you. Take the pendulum in your hands and merge with the pendulum into a uniform being, connecting through your heart. Let the pendulum hang straight down very still and ask that it shows you how a yes-motion swings and then how a no-motion swings. Then start asking your questions. Be sure to ask these so they can be answered with a simple Yes or No! The usual basic rule is counterclockwise circling and swinging along the horizontal line means no. Front and back along the vertical line and clockwise circling means yes. If you want to balance something or clean your room, you can begin a shift in your swing and let the pendulum swing over your subject or room in all directions, with you holding the intention that it is being cleared. Always direct the excess energy to a white fire for the complete transformation.

When I use my pendulum to balance a person after a treatment it swings in big wide circles, like it is collecting and smoothing their auric field.

1. Take a few deep breaths and focus on the task that lies ahead of you. What is taking place is that you show yourself the intuitive sense of yourself, and keep faith that you now are communicating through the pendulum, through your higher self…
∂   If you are looking for answers on behalf of another, then start by connecting and merging the two energy fields into One field, so you can be a truthful channel of information for the other person.
∂   It is important to sense and interpret the movement and the strength of the pendulum swing, it will add some intuitive knowledge. Do not forget that it is the intuitive level of

your consciousness that connects with the energy level, which represents the movement of the pendulum.

∂   The pendulum is a playmate. It is an energy-balancing tool, a key to your intuition and easy to carry with you wherever you go.

Tip! If you want to create your own pendulum instead of buying one, be sure of what you want the pendulum to either represent or how it will be used (cleaning space and people, just for me, etc). Use your intuition and pick out the stones or items you want to use then connect them all and ask if they can work as a team with the same outcome. Be certain of the truth. If there are stones that feel like they do not belong, then pick another one.

CLEANSING WITH FEATHERS & SAGE OR SIMILAR INCENSE

Cleansing or clearing a room or a space is very useful when one self or that space is filled with an unsettling feeling of dirt, despair, too much of other peoples energies, need of a change, etc.

Every room/space has its center point as in where the energy emerges from and spreads out and around. There are a lot of different techniques that one can access to help find this. Since I am more of the intuitive kind of person I will share my method. Be very clear of your intention with the cleansing/change of energy within the space. The clearer you are the better the results that will be achieved.

∂   Why do you want to clear?
∂   What do you expect to accomplish?
∂   Are you ready to "be with the result" when you are done?

1.   You need to create the space/room in your head, the structure of the place, so you are clear where the room ends, where the corners are, etc. "Ask" to feel/see where the center point is placed in the room/space. When you have the image/feeling clear in your mind, picture that from this center point a clear pulsating energy that emerges in all directions. Cleansing means that you make this pulsation go stronger, cleaner and clearer with the help of your tools.
2.   The feather has its own quality (look up the bird and what qualities it holds) that gives it more strength to accomplish/hold energy that can be of help (if you should need any of these qualities in your act). The use of a feather can detect different levels of density in

the air and instead of you using your hand to shatter this density the feather is like your prolonged hand, much more sensitive than your hand though.

3. Sage is a known herb that also helps clearing and cleansing. Light a leaf and use the feather to spread the smoke around in the directions you "feel" is right. The most common sage to use in the purpose of cleansing is the "white sage". As in the little bell that can be helpful if the energy is stagnant, the sound can make the result come quicker.

So to the point ∫
Try to feel the density with the feather in different areas so you know the difference between stagnate and clear air. Then put your intention on clearing away the density and use the feather to "swirl" around – feel the difference after – do the same with some sage. If you work on people it's great to clear their auras after a session. This includes the room you have been working in as well as over the table, etc. There are no limits except for those in one's mind…

TO CLEAN THE ENERGIES OUT OF A ROOM

… also called space clearing
You might need to cleanse a space

∂   When there has been a treatment and there has been a lot of release
∂   When there has been a party
∂   When you have had a quarrel with someone
∂   When you have had a bad day and have transformed a lot of garbage that seems to float around in the air, and you are expecting company in an hour
∂   When you arrive in a hotel room and it feels cluttered. And not just physically!

1. Relax your mind and body and imagine that there is a White Fire burning beside you.
2. Exhale out through your heart and surround your body with the white light, connect to Your source of truth and centre yourself.
3. Inhale and exhale and ensure your body is in balance with your mind and then bring yourself back to the awareness of your task, cleaning with the support of the white fire.
∂   If you want to clean a room, ask the room to show you where its centre is (if you feel you cannot trust that, you can decide). Imagine the White fire expanding and transforming the energies that need to be cleansed. The procedure is the same for cleansing an item.
∂   If you are feeling tired, stressed, angry, sad or not in balance, you can also put yourself into the fire and imagine that this frustrated energy is transformed.

∂ Sometimes it may feel like it is not cleansed enough. In such a case change your intention and your focus and ask the White Fire to transform as much as possible and then connect with the energies remaining and ask for a picture, sense, whatever you can understand so you can cleanse it in a different way. Maybe there is something that needs to be taken care of before the full transformation is done.

CREATING YOUR OWN ALTAR

For me the idea of an altar is to create a place, a space permanent or in the Now, where I can display and collect my favorite tools. A space for items that matter and hold my space, that have profound meaning for me, and where I can show my appreciation for Earth and all my lovely friends…

You can carry items with you in a medicine bag or bundle that can resemble a portable altar. If you are traveling you will most probably want some of your special items with you. The picture shows a "mesa" (table altar or equivalent with a medicine bundle), it is very common in the Andean medicine tradition, and it is said that the Mesa contains the essence of the bearer and it is the most necessary tool for a healer, a person that moves energies…

It is all up to your liking. It is a way of showing grace and to respect your own beliefs and your source. Items have different meanings for each individual. I will give you some guidelines that will spark your own creativity.

∂ A beautiful cloth or bag to put your tools in if you carry them with you
∂ Pen and Paper for writing
∂ Compass to work with the different directions
∂ Salt to clean items or as a symbol for cleansing
∂ A cup or a beautiful glass to use in ceremonies, representing the Female element
∂ A knife, to use as a cutter when you want to disperse and brake off energy strands, cutting branches or herbs, drawing symbols, representing Male power
∂ Mirror for scrying or as a representation of Spirit, your own reflection
∂ Bowl to burn and or to throw away things in
∂ Stones for different purposes
∂ Essential oils like jasmine and rosewood that can represent the elements, emotions or just be as an enhancer
∂ Bowl where you can pour water or other liquids in

Element representations

∂   Earth element: sand or earth, nuts
∂   Water element: shells
∂   Wind element: feathers, incense to show appreciation or to disperse energy
∂   Fire element: candles of different colors that you have initiated (or intended?) for special purposes.

Magical items

Unicorn horn, a wand, a snake skin, dragon tooth, a claw from a jaguar, a vase with fresh flowers which you charged for a particular purpose….

In my home I have a corner in my bookshelf where I have some of my lovely friends. In the room where I work there are a couple of shelves where I have my working tools. When I do a ceremony in nature, I bring some items with me from home, like a special crystal, maybe fruit when I give thanks to Gaia. Then I collect flowers, feathers, seeds etc that I find along the walk to the place I am to create the ceremony at. When I am done with my ceremony I leave behind an altar that will be cared for by nature as in the animals will feast of the fruit and seeds, the wind will carry the feathers. If I do open meditations, I create an altar for the occasion that supports me to hold space and enhance the experience.

A LITTLE FUN IN THE IMPORTANCE OF COLOURS

I see colours as vivid fairies, that I merge, play and enjoy, and usually I carry an intention with them.
All colours merge into the colour white. You provide vibrations in different ways, both within and outside yourself. You can wear clothes in certain colours for certain intentions. Food and drink can have a corresponding frequency in a balanced combination or setting at the table, as in coloured plates and glasses, pots and pans. Take a bath in colored salt and add some coloured "water resistant" crystals to add some extra vibration. There are many words connected to colours, this is an easy, fun way to start to play with them, enjoy!

Red wisdom

∂   Dynamics, celebration, deep energy, warmth, courage, masculine energy, blood holds a grounded frequency

- ∂ Interior; Increases activity, lessens concentration.
- ∂ Clothes; Vitality, passion, lust, strength
- ∂ Bathe with a red colour or a red stone
- ∂ Red makes you warm if you are frozen, tired, exhausted

Orange wisdom

- ∂ Inspiration, action, insight, desire to work, sex, relationships, dynamic
- ∂ Interior; Evening, study, a feast where the table is set in orange becomes a successful party
- ∂ Clothes; An interest and concern for humans, liberated, wear orange underwear if you have problems with your period and in the Andean culture, orange brings you abundance.
- ∂ Bath; Balances eczema, allergies, and increases your feminine energy.

Yellow Wisdom

- ∂ Inviting, clarity, joy, power, vulnerability
- ∂ Interior; Learning, being able to focus
- ∂ Clothes; Optimistic personality and in Peru luck and prosperity.
- ∂ Bath; Joy, digestion, weight problem

Green wisdom

- ∂ Green, stands for the love of nature, animals, the earth. Harmony, healing, calms the heart, muscle nerves, love, compassion
- ∂ Interior; Bedroom, kitchen, practice
- ∂ Clothes; Sturdy, practical, efficient, kind
- ∂ Bath; Calm & Balanced, good before important meetings

Turquoise wisdom

- ∂ New future communications (with ourselves) in the first place
- ∂ Interior; Be bold!
- ∂ Clothes; Broad, yet alert, a little mysterious, freedom, change
- ∂ Bath; Concentrate on one's self, followed by clarity

Blue wisdom

- ∂ Stillness, relaxation, care, clarity, communication
- ∂ Interior; Relaxation, makes small rooms look bigger
- ∂ Clothes; Control, uniforms, freedom, change
- ∂ Bath; Good for the neck, sleep, headache

Indigo wisdom

- ∂ Intuition, understanding, mysticism, meditation
- ∂ Interior; Creative work, family
- ∂ Clothes; Radical, individualistic, unconventional
- ∂ Bath; Good for the ears, skin, sleep

Violet wisdom

- ∂ Spiritual consciousness, art, imagination, creativity
- ∂ Interior; Theatre, classroom, play, media
- ∂ Clothes; Dreams, individualistic, unconventional
- ∂ Bath; Peace fullness

MANTRA, USING YOUR VOICE

I came in contact with mantras when I started practicing Kundalini yoga. They have beautiful mantras created for mostly every issue the body and mind can come up with, mostly connected with a physical motion. You sing them between 3-11 minutes. There are some specific ones that you sing for an hour for special occasions. Me being Me, I had to try just how powerful these words and motions were, so I could use them and recommend them to my clients and students. I prepared myself. My intention was clear. I was tired of having too many paths to choose from. I wanted just one path to walk upon. I started to sing and move my arms, pump my navel back and forth, and "saw" my three paths. My first task was to get it to be one path. That was fairly easy, but I had not anticipated the size of the one path. It was massive. And then I realized that I had to really be focused to achieve my intent. I sang and I sang and I sang for 4 hours. I cleansed out a massive amount of energy and stirred up motions not only within me, as there were scratches on the windows, candles falling down and the light was flickering. If there were some spirits trying to put me off the task, well I just got more stubborn and continued. Today, I am sure that my Higher Self, my better half, was trying to get me to relax a little, since I ended up with fever and I was unable to move for three days. I just laughed and admitted to myself that maybe, just maybe I overdid it and it was not to be recommended to others. But I had one path and a cleansed seat of will and after the ordeal with the fever I felt great. My teacher looked at me with a mix of "Is she crazy?" and concern. I can highly recommend using mantras as a tool for connecting with yourself and merging your body and mind.

My story of the word mantra

Comes from India, meaning something like "the mind can free itself from restrictions." Man means mind. Traj means to be free from bonds. According to and freely translated from a Buddhist perspective, there are people – the "seers" – who can be in contact with both heaven and earth. The purpose of mantras is to "come to terms with the divine," serving like a magnet to attract the spiritual energies you seek to dance with. Another interpretation is this: A mantra straightens out the relationship between the finite self and the infinite self, to manifest your intention so that destiny can be fulfilled

Mantra can also be seen as a lens for which vibration you want to embrace your life with.

Mantras are a fantastic tool. They open your voice and therefore ease the way for your communication within and without, and it strengthens your will and your endurance. Choosing mantras with a specific content will support you and attract what you need to move forward. You will feel that you radiate in a different vibration when you are in the swirls of these vibrations and then can be able to give some of that vibration to others.

A mantra has a specific wavelength, a certain frequency, with a clear demonstrable and positive effect on both body and mind. It is the combination of sound, resonance and rhythm that produces the increased awareness and directs your flow of thoughts in a specific way.

The power of the mantra increases the more you use it and the more aware you are as an individual. Mantra is a technical device to regulate and simultaneously control the mind to finally just be. A mantra vibration harmonize with your super strings (your own sensory instrument), causing them to vibrate and merge into a beautiful melody. When a mantra is performed properly it stimulates different glands in the brain; the hypothalamus, pituitary and pineal gland. They work together to secrete hormones there, which are sent throughout the body, and in turn create the balance that mantra is for. When you repeat a mantra, it is important that you move your mouth and if there is an indication touch your tongue very precise on a certain place in your mouth, that will stimulate the reflex points you have on your tongue and in the palate, follow that suggestion.

Each mantra has its importance. The words mean something, but it's the word vibration that has power and that tunes the instrument. Of course, the words also have their importance.

They are positive affirmations that over time affect your self-image and create stillness within. When you sing a mantra, it is not unusual to begin to yawn. Don't be embarrassed. It is used-up, stagnated energy emitting from your body, yawn and continue to sing. Until you find your favourite mantras why not

begin with a simple Aum. It is a wonderful way to set the energies for your day and to finish your day. It connects the whole body and brings you where your intention is being set.

One ancient tradition of AUM

The loveliest explanation of OM is found within the ancient Vedic and Sanskrit traditions. We can read about AUM in the marvellous Manduka Upanishad, which explains the four elements of AUM as an allegory of the four planes of consciousness.

∂ "A" (pronounced "AH" as in "father") resonates in the centre of the mouth. It represents normal waking consciousness, in which subject and object exist as separate entities. This is the level of mechanics, science, logical reason, the lower three chakras. Matter exists on a gross level, is stable and slow to change.

∂ Then the sound "U" (pronounced as in "who") transfers the sense of vibration to the back of the mouth, and shifts the allegory to the level of dream consciousness. Here, object and subject become intertwined in awareness. Both are contained within us. Matter becomes subtle, more fluid, rapidly changing. This is the realm of dreams, divinities, imagination, the inner world.

∂ "M" is the third element, humming with lips gently closed. This sound resonates forward in the mouth and buzzes throughout the head. (Try it.) This sound represents the realm of deep, dreamless sleep. There is neither observing subject nor observed object. All are one, and nothing. Only pure consciousness exists, unseen, pristine, latent, covered with darkness. This is the cosmic night, the interval between cycles of creation, the womb of the divine Mother.

∂ This brings us to the fourth sound of AUM, the primal "unstruck" sound within the silence at the end of the sacred syllable. In fact, the word "silence" itself can be understood only in reference to "sound." We hear this silence best when listening to sound, any sound at all, without interpreting or judging the sound. Listening fully, openly, without preconceptions or expectations. The sound of music, the sound of the city, the sound of the wind in the forest. All can give us the opportunity to follow the path of sound into the awareness of the sound behind the sound.

SOUND AND CHANTING TO YOUR CHAKRAS

When I started to wear my Star, my pentagram, the energy took me on a ride that lasted several years, during which time my body has had to adjust to this form on all levels. I swirled around and was acting out of my ordinary Me until I realized that I was being attuned with this energy and could start to dance with it instead of escaping. It was for me a natural way to start working with geometrical forms, especially in meditations or if I wanted to enhance any mantra song/exercise. Singing or chanting in forms really took off when I had healing courses and every month we worked through one geometrical form and how we could dance with its energy.

Sound is a powerful tool in our lives. From when we are born we are expected to make a sound to show our presence in the world. If we don't, the assumption is that there is something unbalanced within us. Sounds can be overwhelming. It creates vibrations in our body that can be pleasant or unpleasant. Some of us need sounds to clear our minds, or rather make our minds sound less while we are doing something hard *(I know that when I am working through something that is released in my physical body and it is a bit of a struggle, I put my earplugs in with different music. It makes my mind dance and leaves my body alone to release what is needed)*. Sounds can alter moods, make your feel strong or weak, release tensions, evoke feelings and increase energy flow in your bodies (subtle and physical). The vibration of sounds is a core brick for us. It is in our DNA. It vibrates inside of us. Whether we think about it or not, sounds make a difference in our lives and how we behave. (I, for one, cannot be in trance music for very long, the vibrations make me feel nauseous and gives me a very unpleasant feeling).

Give some thoughts to the following questions

∂   How come we usually give more attention to a person who carries a steady and pleasant tone in their voice? We seem to prefer a person who makes sounds; than a person who has no voice. Why is that so???

∂   Do you feel more vulnerable to certain sounds when you are sick?

∂   Do you prefer certain sounds when you are cleaning the house?

∂   What is your preferred music, have you ever thought of why?

Start paying attention to details when it comes to sound and be clearer in how it affects your daily life.

∂   What makes you happy? What makes you stressed out? What gives you a rush of freedom?

∂   Choose some songs that evoke physical sensations such as drums, water, flutes that sound like the wind, etc, and feel the difference and how the sound affects you.

∂   Think about how it feels being in a restaurant at rush hour, where everyone is gathered at the same time and the volume increases. How does this affect you? How does it affect your digestion?

Sounds can be used to heal and to balance, like when you use your voice in chanting for example. There are sounds for each chakra and the organs connected to it, and if you tune these sounds it becomes like a sound meditation with the aim to create space and as a result it gives you and your body a relaxed and uplifted feeling within. You will find that this is a nice and comfortable way to balance yourself.

Sound balancing

Lam	root chakra
Vam	navel chakra
Ram	solar plexus chakra
Yam	heart chakra
Ham	throat chakra
Om	third eye chakra
Aum	crown chakra

I suggest that you start with the root chakra sound. It is more grounding and will give you a good foundation working with the upper chakra sounds. When you are at the crown and chant Aum, before you end let the sound vibrate throughout your whole body, from feet to head.

1. Lie down and feel your body. Is there any tension or feeling of discomfort?
2. Place yourself in a comfortable position. Find your centre, find your pace with your breath and let your light shine throughout your heart and fill your whole body and auric field.
3. Focus on each energy point on each sound, place your hands on the energy point or just visualizing each centre as you chant. Creating a physical connection with your body adds and enhances your sensory system and makes you dance with the whole of You…

4. Start chanting and repeat the sound at least five times. Feel the sensations the sound creates within you.

5. When you have chanted all the chakra sounds, just sit in stillness until all the vibrations have stopped and you feel that you are in total balance within.

Before you return to the "world" again, lie down and feel how the vibration of sounds has balanced your physical body from when you started.

GEOMETRICAL FORMS AND HEALING VIBRATIONS

In this chapter I have been inspired from a book called The Healers manual by Ted Andrews.
Everything contains its own energy, that we know. Have you ever thought about using geometric forms to support you in your healing? Try to sit in the shape of a triangle and let the sound of bells travel around. Place a person in the middle and ask them how it felt. If the person who wants support cannot be present, you can place a photo in the middle instead.

The symbol that holds an overall balancing effect on our body and all connected to it, is the **The square**. You enter a core energy, similar to the core energy that our own body holds that many says is the strand of Life force within. Think structure, steadfast and grounded.

The circle - The Full Moon holds the most natural form in the world. It builds energy spirals of wholeness when you use it together with tuning. It harmonizes all of the bodily systems. It enhances the sound and creates more vitality and energy. It builds a spiral between the Source and the inner "us". Having focus on the Sun and the Moon during a chant you can also link in these two elements into the healing. Think balance.

As a link between our 4 energies we hold; physical, mental, emotional and the spiritual **The cross** is a form that can be used to direct the four elements in the body: fire, water, earth and air. If you sing out from the centre point of the cross, it give the heart a strong boost of energy. It also creates a balanced polarity to the body's electromagnetic field. Think balance between heaven and earth, throughout your body.

In its form **The Half Moon** enhances the power of healing. The form is linked to your throat chakra and by this your ability for clear and hopefully hearty communication. If we need to give our feminine energy a boost using the form of half Ms. Moon is excellent. Think clear communication, between the worlds, your inner self and your outer self.

The triangle enhances and intensifies the energies from the tunes. It can be used to heat up or cool down a person's energy system. It has a strong cleansing effect on the body, any part of us that needs a little cooling down or a boost of the immune system will benefit from the use of the triangle. Think release.

The pentagram, a 5 pointed star is balancing, grounding and a great space holder. If you look at the form as the symbol of our body (head up, arms to the sides and legs) you can easily tune in-to the area that needs a boost or the opposite. It forms a concentrated force of energy which when being used in tuning can bring you closer to your Source. It has a strong connection with the feminine energy and Earth. Think grounding in Self.

When you need to link together your heart and mind using the symbol of a **Hexagram, a 6 pointed sta**r works very smoothly. This form show us how to reach a more straight path between the subtle energies and the physical world, by working strongly on your third eye and your heart chakra. Think the merge between the Divine, our Source with our Selves, our body.

The seven pointed star also called the **Star of St. Bridgette**, a very good symbol for healing and protection in all forms. Holding seven as a sacred number, 7 chakras, 7 subtle bodies and so forth it holds the power to create a vortex that can invoke the energies of our closest 7 planets (if we want to take a dance in Space). Think transformation.

The **Heart** is a form that we all have a strong connection towards. To draw a heart and to write one's intention within and then sing and merge the physical heart to the drawn one is strong and very effective. Think about the force behind the power of LOVE.

You can use stones, flowers, candles, whatever you find that correlates with you in creating a geometric form. If you wish to enhance an element into the form you are bringing in the, elements too. You can place yourself inside the circle of items and just sit in the energy of the form. You can use the form to enhance you when singing mantras, making or creating affirmations and prayers. It is only your mind that can restrict you in how to be supported by these forms. There are many other forms that you can work with as well, and it might be that you find your favourite one that you have your source connection with.

Suggestion; The Moon is full and you feel overloaded by emotions. Find items that symbolize the sea, as in seashells. Place them around you in a circle, so you can direct your "water" in-to the shells. Inside them you create a five-star Pentagram the symbol for your physical body, which you lit up with five candles. And in the nearest space where you sit you draw a triangle, the symbol for your Mind, Soul and Spirit, here you can place crystals that symbolizes these three parts of you. Have your intention clear in your mind and start to start to tune, sing or talk. Be present. Be aware of where the motions arise from. Breathe, fall in-to your own existence…

CHAPTER 4

THE BODY

THE BODY

Care with gentleness
Dare to be vulnerable
Hold her / him gently
Be proud

It is so easy to forget that we only have one body and it is supposed to last the whole way through. Whatever new path you will walk upon, whatever old path you are about to close down, make sure that you bring your body with you. You don't want to leave it behind or on a sidetrack. About living in the Now, the body is here, present, part of your awareness all the time. The deeper you and your Body bond, the better flow in your daily life you will experience.

I have really come to love and respect My body. Throughout my life up to the year I had spinal surgery I thought of my body as a tool for my convenience. It has always been strong, flexible and open for new adventures. It has also suffered a lot because of me not wanting to release old patterns, and it has really tried to get me back on track. I was a poor listener. Finally, a really old pattern came to the surface with the result that I had to undergo surgery in my spine. For the first time in my life I had my body as a companion, not a partner. I have to admit I am happy that I had to experience this transmission. It has made me a more understandable person in many ways and not only towards myself.

When I became a body therapist I was already working with energies, so I had a smooth way into the core of the muscles and what needed to be worked on. I have always had the utmost trust that The Body knows more than me (except my own), and my job was to follow the directions my clients' bodies gave me. I loved it. It was like a joyride every time. I never knew where I was being lead during a session but the end result was always perfect for the client. I have always used my body as a "back up information tool" so I could follow what happened to the other person's body through my own body. I experienced the shifts, the swirls and the movements happening with my client. It helped my confidence and was a smart move from "my Source" since it directed me towards letting the Bodies be the therapist and I the spokesperson for them. I loved them (the bodies) even more for letting me inside their sanctuary and giving me their trust.

Over the years my Body and I have experimented a lot, from drinking colloidal silver and gold by the litres, to making my Body become as ethereal as it can be without vanishing from its earthly manners, singing mantras for hours and covering myself with crystals. I mean, how can my clients trust me if I have not endured the act beforehand? Off course we all have different constitutions, but we do live in a Body that has the same content.

My Body and I have really undergone journeys together, and I am impressed that she never lacks interest in playing, of learning other ways to do things (or is it me…) and the encouragement she has given me in being so receptive and being able to present my ideas, intentions and make them into reality. There is one incident that I would like to share. I had often heard about those stories where the mother lifted the car to save her child, etc. On one level I had admiration for these people, how did they create their bodies to do all these fantastic acts? But since I am not a mum, it felt out of my reach to experience anything remotely similar to these stories, until I had my surgery and had to see how far my own belief system ran.

Sometime after the surgery my body started to be aware that there were foreign items placed inside it: titanium screws, big, strong and very different material from the bones of a spine. The protests from the body were strong. I was in pain and needed to understand the difference between the healing pains and the "get the screws out of my spine" pains. I asked my body what picture she could give me that explained how the spine saw herself in my body. I was presented with a picture of an empress and really laughed and had to admit it was a good picture, she is an empress, she holds up the whole body. She was in distress. She had a very vain personality, knew her importance and liked to be admired for that, and having foreign objects in her domain was not ideal. I came to the conclusion that she is vain, she likes her own image, and she needs to keep this image to do her work with excellence. So my intention was to remove all pain that had do with the screws and only keep what was a part of the healing phase. I visualized this room of utmost beauty, everything my empress needed she could find there, I transformed my 6 screws into mirrors all over the room. I then invited my empress (my spine) into this new room and she was amazed and flattered. I told her to examine her feeling that there were imposters (my screws) in her environment. if she took a look at how they looked maybe she would change her mind?

She went to the mirrors and what did she see? Herself in glory, she went to all six of them and since she couldn't find any fault with herself, she couldn't find any fault with the feeling of the imposters. I am serious when I say that this whole event took a maximum of 10 minutes, 95 percent of my pain dissolved, and I was left with my healing pain. That pain has never returned. The Body is a fantastic companion and she was as happy as I was. She does not like to be in agony either. So I figured out the way to create. She knows how to act it out. We are a perfect couple.

The biggest lesson I learned is that pushing my Body too much, ends in a break. Something will snap inside. It doesn't matter if it's an emotional, physical or spiritual snap. If I don't dance alongside my Body and allow this denser part of my being to decide the pace of our journey... well I can tell you this: I wished someone had told me when I started actively with this line of awareness and work that if I would have carried myself with more patience, my journey would go ahead faster. I do, however, ask my Body when I feel that my patience has reached its limits and I am getting bored if I can take a little etheric journey out of her. Since I ask, my Body is prepared and allows me to travel far and beyond and stretch all limits on many levels of my being. She knows that I am returning, so she holds space for me patiently until my dance in the realms are done for that time... My Body allows me to shape shift to animals, to walk for hours in nature, encourages me to stretch a little deeper, have her as an instrument and tool during my work, dance for hours and hours, express my emotions, and it knows how to approach both people and nature so we are all in comfort. I hope I will have time to learn a lot more from her.

Tip: If you haven't found a way to communicate on a level of comfort with your body, ask the Body what she believes is the best way for you to create a stronger bond of trust and playfulness between you. She knows you. She knows your abilities as well as limits, but she also knows how to move around your limitations the smoothest ways, without taking shortcuts. You will find that you have had the best dancing partner in you always.....

Daily self care

Be gentle with yourself. Whatever level you are exploring with your bodies (physical and etheric), there will be a cleanse. For every door you open inside you, there is need of a sweep and awareness of the process you are in, what organs are effected, what emotions are being brought up to the surface and more. Ask your Body how she can be aided. More water, movements, rest? And you will find yourself dancing within the smoother outcome.

How do emotions affect our Body

Emotions do effect our body. The saying "I feel like I have butterflies in my tummy", when you are nervous, that is an emotion. Feeling like you are in a rollercoaster when you are to do a presentation which really means a lot to you, well, that is an emotion. Have fire coming out of your eyes when you are really furious, emotions. Our body is great by letting us feel / see "metaphors", so it's easier for us to understand what is going on with us.

Here are some methods to be able to trace the core effect of what emotions create within you. Start to distinguish each and every one of them, so you can work on the effects separately with the aim to "own" your expression fully. Then you are standing in your most aware power and can act out from a different level of your consciousness.

∂   To be more in tune with what is happening within, be aware of how and which muscles get affected, (knots in the tummy, clinching jaws, skin rashes etc).
∂   Does the feeling affect your breathing ability and your voice?
∂   Does the feeling affect the way you watch out for yourself? Are you more alert suddenly or do you care less about your whereabouts?
∂   Do you suddenly just watch romantic or horror movies?

Think about how you are acting out, both towards yourself and others. If there are emotions we hold on to and refuse to let go, many times we can injure ourselves, to let the steam out of the system. So please be fully aware and talk to your body.

THE BELT AND THE PLUG

Our brain is a wonderful tool that loves to play and has this ability to not know what is reality and what is not. That is why using visualization is so effective and when you add that the outcome is something the brain already recognizes, success is a fact.

For me, on my path, it is very important to walk side-by-side with my body, preferably at the same time. When I ask my mind to create an intent having to do with my body, it seems to be really easy if I choose very simple pictures, something that my brain can already refer to, there is no need to reinvent it if it is already created and has a meaning attached to it. You know how it feels when you have eaten too much food and you can finally open your belt, unzip, and let it all out, ahhh, this is a feeling your body knows as an imprint of relief. When you create intentions that correlate with your body find the simple ones. Working with my own body and other people's, I usually come across a muscle, connective tissue, an organ that seems to be tight or headaches etc. The body might have kept something locked in for years that are now ready to be released. If the body has been holding onto something for a while, it believes that this is the way it should be. This is its creation. It can be tough to release these contractions and make them stay relaxed until you get the awareness about them and can work on them in the "moment" your body chooses to bring them back.

The outcome of this exercise is that your body should feel freer, that you find it's more spacious within. Sit in mediation and ask your body to show you how it looks inside, so you get accustomed to being inside yourself. Look at anatomy pictures, so you know where all the organs and other internal parts reside within you. Breathe through your body, be inside your bones, feel the water inside, be in your heart and feel the heartbeat. Let your imagination flow free and play...

1. Imagine a situation that always makes you feel bloated. Go a little deeper within and locate the exact place where it feels like you are "pumped up" and bring your focus to that place.
2. Imagine that this body part is tied up and you have to untie it. In your imagination you open it up, loosen the knots, do whatever it feels like it needs and feel how the body relaxes and the feeling of being bloated disperses.
3. Sometimes it can be more efficient to open up like a ventilation plug and let the energy that is locked in to flow away freely (preferable into a white transformative fire).

LOCATING THE CORE IN YOUR BODY

In anatomy when you are talking about your core, it has to do with muscles you need to strengthen to keep yourself in a good stance. The major muscles are in and around your mid and lower back and moves up through the spine to keep you straight. There is no slumping shoulders and hunched back if you are carrying a good core. When I talk about core I am also considering the etheric core that you will find as a line just in front of your spine and behind your heart. It can be a little difficult to feel it fully, so visualize it until you are integrated with the feel of it.

After doing Kundalini yoga since 1997 and working with the spinal energy, the feeling still took me by surprise when I felt this strong current in my back, after I had my surgery, it was not in any way related to my physical spine, an impressive feeling.

Here is a nice exercise that will bring you into your body in a nice way;

1. Dare to feel every part of your body without relying on your mind to give you the answers you seek.
2. When you have found the core within your body, expand your inner light from that place and let that light travel around you as a companion and around all of your bodies. If you are to dance, better get to know your dance partner.

3. Return to your core with your heart and visualize that you are a shimmering periscope, move out from your heart out in your arms aiming for a finger, feel and see how it looks and feels on the way.

∂ When you have reached the fingertip, open an eye-lid and peek out. What do you see?

4. Move around your whole body like this. Take a look inside your organs, ride in your veins, glide on your connective tissue, move with your imagination and your unlimited mind. Have fun!!

A BALANCING AND STRENGTHENING MEDITATION FOR YOUR RIGHT AND LEFT HALVES OF YOUR BRAIN

1. Sit in comfort with your legs crossed.
2. Breathe long deep breaths during the exercise.
   Inhale and at the same time rise up to a standing position with your legs still crossed.
3. When you come up, you bring your arms back to stretch your chest and open up your heart and lungs. If you have a problem with raising, maybe you can come up on your knees and from there work yourself up to a standing position in time. *It can be nice to sit on something soft for your knees.* Exhale as you sit down
4. Repeat
5. Do this exercise for 3-7 minutes.

mba

THE CONNECTIVE TISSUE

The connective tissue protects and holds the entire internal world inside our body. I see it as one piece "leotard" with no openings for head or feet. For me the connective tissue has always been the "one" delivering the intention, the messenger when I have perceived movements inside the body, mine or another persons. Connective tissue, or fascia, is what has made me able to trace the root cause in a body. I now know that the "roads" I see inside a body is what they today call myofascial trains.

While reading the next lines try to get a visual picture as well as understanding it with your mind. Connective tissue transports electricity, and the meridian system is placed in the outermost part of the connective tissue. The connective tissue is found everywhere inside the body and can be seen as the primary "bearer" of our intention, "the means" that brings our intention into action". The network of meridians can be seen as the channels that connect our sensory system to the body's sensations and wisdom. The meridians receive their information from all of our sensory systems and in their close contact with the fascia the impulses are instant.

Our ethereal body is in its absolute. It is connected with our physical body, and will not be dissolved until the physical body dies (if ever). From one perspective we can define the meridians as one vital part of the structure of the etheric body, a link that connects us with our source. Spiritual dis-eases can be said to be transmitted over to the etheric meridian structure before it anchors in the physical structure. Fascia, binds specific cells into tissue and those tissues into organs to hold the bodily systems in place). It connects muscles to bones and joints, surrounds every nerve and every vessel, connects all internal structures safely in their specific place and embraces the body in its whole. Fascia is the one thing that holds all of these cables and anchors together. Every part of the body is in connection through the fascia. Fascia contains water, every little strand of tissue holds a lot of water. Fascia is the system that is the main transporter for the life force, Ki, throughout the body. The internal liquids in the fascia that move in and out through the lymphatic and capillary system are also seen as one vital part in the life force – Ki (Chi).

The lymphatic system

For me the lymphatic system is one to hold very dear. It is the system that will ultimately help to rid all the energy waste that I have been collecting. I can see when my system isn't at its peak, I get more cellulites and feel bloated. To aid the system, I dry brush, drink more water than usual and contemplate on opening up my blockages.

This system works in connection with the fascia, since its job is to maintain the correct fluid balance in the tissues and blood. The system defends the body against disease, conserves protein and removes bacteria and other cellular waste products. It is an imbricate filtering system made up of tiny lymph vessels, which circulate milky fluid called lymph throughout the body. The movement of lymph is affected by the massage-like action of surrounding muscles, since the lymphatic system has no pump such as the heart to propel it. Lymph vessels carry excess fluid and bacteria from the tissues, which are then filtered out by lymph nodes or glands in the course of circulation. These nodes also produce the white blood cells known as lymphocytes. They are located along the vessels, rather like beads on a string. Clusters of nodes are found in the neck, armpits, groin and knees as well as down the middle of the torso.

TRAPPED IN A WEB

This is a way I have found quick and easy, when life has presented me with too many question marks and I feel trapped into a web. It gives me a little breather, so I can re-group my mind, my senses and my body, and try again…

When you do not understand what somebody says, do not struggle to understand each word

∂   Stop the attempt!
∂   Silence yourself within and listen with your inner ear (as you would listen with your inner senses).

When you are puzzled by what you see or hear, do not try to understand.

∂   Place yourself a little on the side and be quiet for a while!
∂   When you are calm the complicated things seem simple to interpret.

To understand what happens, do not push, open to the unexpected and be aware.

∂   See without staring.
∂   Listen quietly instead of listening intensely.
∂   Use intuition and reflection instead of trying to figure out an answer for everything.

ASSEMBLE YOUR ENERGY IN A QUICK AND POWERFILLED EXERCISE

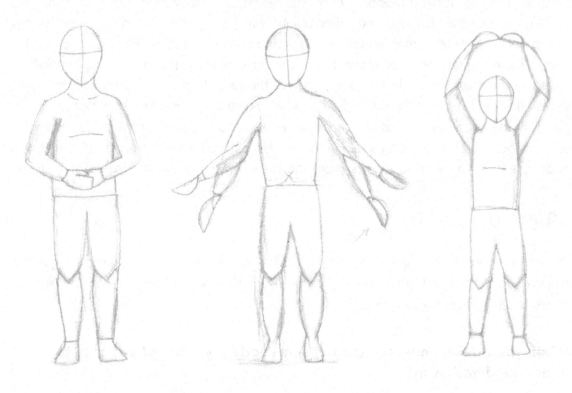

This is powerful exercise that has the ability to get you focused, grounded and stilled in some minutes. It requires some space for your body to move freely and preferably it shall be performed where you feel that the roof is not on top of your head.

1. Inhale, summon yourself. Let your body and mind merge and exhale out through your heart. Stand firm with knees slightly bent.
2. Inhale and at the same time and pace as your breath start lifting your arms (keep them straight at your sides with your palms facing down). Imagine that you collect energy from the Earth into your palms.
3. When you get in line with your navel, turn your palms facing up and while your palms are moving together, imagine that the energy collected from Earth will merge and balance the two sides of your brain.
4. When your arms reach above your head, collect energies from Heaven and form the arms into a circle with your palms facing downward.

5. Exhale and at the same time move your energy-filled palms downward just in front of your face and along the front of your body. I always imagine that I press down the energy like through a tube (my body).
6. When you reach the height of your navel, place your hands on top of your navel and feel how the energy you have just received is being stored in this centre.

Repeat the movement until you feel that you are in balance and safe throughout your body…

DNA MEDITATION

Intention with this meditation is for your body to develop into a higher potential in your own creation, in your life.

1. Be in comfort. Breathe and turn your intention towards the core of your inner heart.
2. What color does your heart carry today? Let that color merge with the rest of your bodies and continue to breathe until you feel you are in total balance.
3. Let your heart connect to your Higher self, when you feel that you are fully merged, imagine yourself (your persona) shrink.
∂ You are becoming smaller and smaller and finally what is left to be seen is your Light of consciousness in the core of all the cells in your body.
4. See yourself as a point of light travelling toward the core of your cells. The core contains your DNA strands, your code of life.
∂ Breathe and re-connect your light with your heart.
5. Ask your DNA strands to release all records, all decisions or beliefs that no longer serve you. *You do not need to know what you are releasing, if there is anything of significance that transforms, you will understand this after the meditation is over.*
6. Through the core of your heart, ignite all your DNA molecules in your body and see yourself "light up."
7. Now, when your cells are filled with bright light, tell your DNA strands that you seek to reach your highest potential in this present life. That you need support from them to bring these new programs, ideas, and thoughts into your life, and enable them to merge with all your bodies.
8. When you feel that you are balanced in all of this re-programming, send your consciousness back into the core of your heart, and imagine it spreading out through your bodies. Feel secure in your decisions, that you will welcome every opportunity to develop into the

highest potential in your own creation, in your life. You have just made a commitment to walk your path, you are ready to really love and cherish yourself and accept whom you are, the light beaming person you already are. Acknowledge the power that resides and dances within your heart. At the end, let a breath emerge from your heart, feel the bubbling new energy filling you up, and creating, in your body, the "space-you-need-for-today". Take three deep breaths with the intention to return to the Now, move your arms and legs, open your eyes, smile and just be.

THE AURA OR WHAT DANCES AROUND OUR BODIES

Me being a very sensitive child, perceived streaks of lights and waves waltzing around and in and out of people. Usually I also noticed how the physical body re-acted when these waves contacted them. Being raised to curtsy and be polite to people when I met them, sometimes it was hard to do that, since my body's reaction was to want to walk away, having seen the dance of these lights and how they could penetrate a person, even if the other person didn't want to receive them and I didn't want these rays of light within me. I have many times walked a long way around an area of town or in the forest if I perceived something that didn't resonate with me that day. I have many times been late for dinner…

I have had a lot of fun with my abilities as well. When having love problems, I would place myself on a bench and watch people in action and tune into those with a shimmering, lovely energy between them, telling myself that, that is how it should look like and feel that within me too.
I have been able to perceive the aura around the cashiers in the supermarket and those that had a vibrant aura, well that was the queue I went in. I guess I worked up a system within myself over the years, created by my own trust and faith in what I perceived. I followed that feeling. What these years of awareness have taught me is that I also create situations around me. Coming late to dinner might not be the way to deal with my sensitivity and therefore I have embraced the fact of sensitivity, and being the person that I am and walk straight into the lion's den instead which has not been so pleasant at times. I remember the first time I saw a colour dancing around a person's body with my physical eyes, wow that was profound. He was giving me change back and suddenly his hands exploded in yellow and I screamed, MOVE YOUR ARM AGAIN, he just stared but got it somehow and then started to dance around and we both shrieked in joy. I was late to my workshop that day, oops. When I get bored, tired, or just slip into my "other Me", I really enjoy the dance of vibrations. I truly encourage you to have some fun and develop your own sensitivities.

OUR SEVEN SUBTLE BODIES

There are many teaching about the fields around our body. Presented below is the way I was taught and how I still see it. I have developed my senses throughout the years, and what differs is more my ability to see "beyond" the colours, the fields but mostly my interpretation. To view the aura and get another perception of it, you can divide the aura in seven layers, your seven subtle bodies. See them as ribbons carrying different types of energy that are fixed at a certain distance from our physical body, as the rings around the planet Saturn. Each of these rings is said to be connected with our soul and its relationship to our physical body. They vary in strength, colour and appearance, and they are all tied to a particular chakra and then an organ and an emotion. When it comes to what colours the etheric fields hold, may vary from person to person. We contain all colours and then we create our own pallet with the variations we need to keep ourselves in balance. *I am also convinced that there are colour-combinations that exist today, which have been developed out of the higher vibration Gaia and we, who live upon her hold today, compared to only 10 years ago.*

Etheric body

Springing from the root chakra, the body is bluish-grey and shimmers in colour. This is the first body and it lies between the physical body and the other six. Its function is to keep a balance between the physical body and the subtle bodies. The etheric body is an exact ethereal copy of our physical body. When our "life force" comes or goes from us, it always passes through this subtle body. It receives stores and transports energy, and spreads the energy into the physical body. It co-ordinates the energy and creates the links between the cells, to make them work as a whole. The etheric force is flexible and creative, gifted with life and power, and it is that which controls our mind and our memory. If the etheric body is out of balance these energies filter down to our physical body and can cause imbalance, illness, etc.

Emotional body

This band of energy is linked to the solar-plexus and our heart chakra. It is lighter than the etheric body, and can be likened to multi-coloured clouds in constant movement. It dances tightly with the etheric body, and these two together balance our emotions as a reflector, allowing us to feel the energy of other people's emotions. Positive emotions of love and happiness improve and enhance its colour and shimmer. Negative emotions seem to add a layer on top of the bodies. When in balance you will feel you have a strong sense of emotional strength and mental stability.

Mental body

This energy band is a vibrating shade of pale yellow, varying in tone depending on the mental activity you are in, it seems to shine brighter than the etheric body. This mental energy gets people to think more clearly and act more rationally. It contains the structure of our thoughts and ideas, creates and perceives pictures, imaginations, ideas, and gives us focus. Many thoughts passes our mind per day, every thought is energy.

A strong mental body keeps your mind merged with your body so they can aid each other in the overall task of separating the mind-worms and the truth, keeping a healthy balance within. Frustration in this body blocks our expelling organs, especially the kidneys. Stress in the body results in a build up of toxins in the physical body that can manifest as allergies, for example. In addition, mental stress and tension tend to be stored in our muscles.

Astral body

More intense, soft multi-coloured, the astral body is also linked to the solar plexus and heart chakra. It contains our whole personality. When the body is in balance, the individual usually has an intuitive feel for things and events in life and can sometimes even see into the future. The astral body is working to compare all the "past-life" experiences (can also be what happened yesterday) and keep this knowledge from intervening in our daily lives in this present incarnation or NOW, so mistakes aren't' repeated or that lessons will be learned …

Causal body

Crystal-clear and intensively blue, this body is linked to our throat chakra. The causal body is the seat of our willpower. It allows us to fulfil our personal destiny, and so is the gateway to our higher consciousness. This body is responsible for the organization of "past-life" information, before it becomes available to the astral body.

Soul body

Bright, vibrant and golden in colour, this energy is linked with our third eye. It includes our spiritual essence and is in a sense our Higher Self, which allows our soul to wander around freely in / out of our body. This energy band enters through our pineal gland.

Spiritual body

This energy body is a composition of shimmering pastel colors, which are linked to the heart chakra. It represents a combination and fusion of the total subtle anatomy of the physical body. Our body's basic copy-blueprint is used in this body. Its ethereal shell is a kind of surface protection around the subtle bodies, which separates the subtle anatomy of other energies around us. It reflects our true identity and our higher potential, our perspective and our ability to free ourselves from physical limitations in contrast to the ethereal, subtle bodies. We have here a "hot" body that can be likened to a hot spring that goes beyond the etheric body. This heat is generated by a normal cell division and is influenced by our scale of metabolism. It can be said to be a bi-product of our physical activity.

GET TO KNOW YOUR AURA

We all walk around with a big force field around us. Like a sixth sense, it will guide us, make sure we become a little more aware, and get us out of trouble. It is called our auric field. Mystics have always known about it, we in the "world" have recently accepted that there is more to the human body than what the naked eye can see. Time for you to discover about your own aura!
It is your aura that tells you if someone behind your back is staring at you.
It is your Aura that makes you aware that a fierce quarrel has recently ended, since it makes you aware of that the air is still thick and tense, loaded with strong feelings.

Your aura is an extension of your physical body (skin, organs, meridians etc), and works much like an insect's tentacles, or like an antenna.
This force field of light, heat and electromagnetism, ranging from 1 to 3 meters around your body, is your private sphere. The fact that all living things have an aura has been claimed by the mystics throughout history, and now even scientists have found and accepted that these energy fields exist. A number of prominent scientists have developed cameras that make it possible to take pictures of the force field. The camera is called the Kirlian, named after

Semyon Kirlian who in 1939 accidently discovered that if an object on a photographic plate is connected to a high-voltage source, an image is produced on the photographic plate.

A high voltage source could also be visible if a person holds a vibrant energy. That would then be what causes orbs and other light phenomena around a person's body, the auric field.

PLAY YOUR OWN MELODY

Your aura will make you intuitively think of some people and instinctively dismiss others. The expression "to be on the same wavelength" is named more aptly than you think.

Your force field is a unique combination of light, heat and electromagnetic fields in different proportions. If we were able to take an EEG of your aura, the paper printout would show that you have a very special combination of waves. You play your own melody. When you meet another person — regardless of what qualities that person holds — if the two of you hold a different wave pattern, your aura does not like the other person's aura. It will be difficult for the two of you to be in each other's presence. It is like having two radios blasting different songs. Your tunes simply cannot be played simultaneously.

ENERGY FIELDS INTERWEAVE

However, if you meet a person whose aura plays a tune whose frequency is close to yours, you know that you will enjoy yourself in their company. If the melody is appealing enough the tune will soon be playing "love music." If the two of you decide to make love, your energy fields are further intertwined. Intercourse creates a powerful exchange of auric-energies between the people involved. And even in the case of casual sex, the energy from the other person can reside long after you've parted. It's not just sexual encounters that cause auras to intertwine. Every encounter with another person leads to the exchange of energies. You give and you take. In some cases, however, you might feel that you give more than you get back. After meeting with such a person, you can be exhausted. You may feel as though the person "sucked the life out of you," and that is exactly what has happened. But there are ways to shield yourself. To angrily making a stop sign with your hand and say, "Do not come here, you, ehhh aura thief!" is not recommended. The person you turned to would have their eyebrows raised higher than you thought physically possible

FORM A CLOSED CIRCUIT

An easier way is to "turn off" your aura, so that no energy can be given away. Sit down, cross your legs and keep your thumbs and index fingers together. Your body has now formed a closed circuit, and no one will suspect what you have just done.

You can also use breathing as a tool. Take deep breaths through the nose down into the stomach. Visualize that you are breathing out a bright, white light from the core of your body. Each time you exhale, imagine how your aura expands and your aura gets new, vibrant energy with the density you need to have for the rest of your day. But before you can learn how to shield your aura, you must first discover it. Through simple exercises you can learn to pay attention to how your aura is changing. All you need is a little uninterrupted time.

HOW TO IDENTIFY YOUR OWN AURA

An easy way to begin to get to know your aura is by brining your palms together. Breathe in, relax, open up your senses and merge with your heart. Feel the energy pouring from your heart out in your arms and finally ending in your palms. With relaxed and slightly cupped palms, fingers touching, you bring your palms apart from each other. Play with the thought that you have a ball with a lot of bounce in it between your hands and move your hands back and forth without letting go of the bouncy ball. Add your intention to actually "see" the ball being formed in between your palms. It will make it easier. When you feel that you are One with the bouncy ball, continue with the next exercise.

Feel and steer your energy from a longer distance. Your intention is to send heat to the opposite arm. This is a great technique to use if you have any pain in or on your body. Sometimes it is difficult to touch directly on an area of the body. If a person has injured themselves and a mere touch would make them hurt more, this technique can be of good use to ease the pain that lingers in the person's auric field. It is a great way to feel by playing and getting to know the different auric fields.

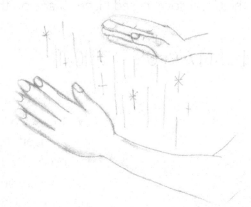

Once you have discovered your own aura, you can make a fun exercise with a friend. Ask your friend to lie down and relax with closed eyes. Place your hand about 7-8 cm above the body and slowly move around the body until you perceive a shift in energy. Hold your hand still and ask your friend to guess where over the body your hand is placed. You will discover that the answer most likely is correct.

AURA RINGS

Imagine that our bodies are surrounded with Hula-Hoops. Each of these hoops holds an emotion that is trapped there. They vary in size, thickness and density. There can be more than one at the same place.

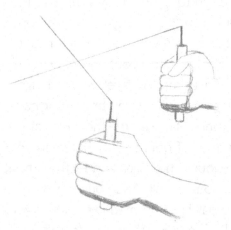

When I started to recognize these hoops, I was curious of why we place Hula-Hoops around ourselves? My belief is that when an emotion has been released and we believe it is cleansed out of our system and life for good, the body and your spirit may have a different view on the cause and want us to be aware and learn from that experience. It can also be that the physical reaction at the time of the release might be too strong to carry so we preserve the release for a while. Usually though we are not in tune with ourselves enough to have a weekly "Hula-Hoop" cleanse so the body will just adapt to this addition and make itself as comfortable as possible and life goes on….

How can you determine that there is a Hula-Hoop around a body? Say that you have worked on a special point and it doesn't seem to let go, release, giving a feeling that something is stuck, etc, a good idea is to get your dowsing or divining rods out, and start checking for rings. If you don't own a pair of rods, they are easily made by bending a pair of metal coat hangers in the shape of the picture. The connection and intention you use with rods are similar to a pendulum, it is the extension of you. When you start working with rods, tune in and connect with the whole of you and be clear of your intent. The thought is that you have the rods in front of you, at hip height.

- ∂   Ask to be told when you meet the person's aura or in this case an aura ring.
- ∂   Relax and walk towards them, then when you come upon a ring, steady your rods and "lift" the ring up and above the head, slip it into the White fire you have beside you and let it transform. The more perception you manage to keep, the better.
- ∂   Ask the body to give you a feel, a picture of what it held and tell the person what you are working on. Then you start over again until you can't find any more rings.
- ∂   Remember that there can be rings within rings, especially if there is a ring around a vital organ such as the liver. There can be emotions pouring out from the liver if the person has worked to release a lot of anger, fear and frustration. It can be a good idea to take a second look.

If you don't have any rods or hangers, you can use your hands. It will take some extra time to extend them. Visualize that the energy from your hands will come out and turn into rods.

SEE THE COLORS IN THE AURA

Within us, we have the capacity to expand our vision beyond what we thought possible. The grass may be more vibrant green, the sky more intense blue, the fine details much clearer. By training your eyes, it is assumed that we can also learn to see other people's auras and colours in and around them.

Each aura holds a rainbow of colours. One colour usually dominates and that colour is said to represent the person's primary personality. Some other colours may be seen as weaker or flicker in and out. You can then benefit by looking at the properties and gaining an understanding of these colours, to balance your body and mind.

To practice and start trusting what you perceive may take some time. It takes time to tune in to your body and mind and heighten your sensibility and to trust what you feel within.

For example, if you have just meditated for several days you are bound to carry more white and purple and green in your aura. You may want to add a little red to come back to us on earth.

I would also like to mention that you can see an aura different ways. You can see the colours with your physical eyes but it is also very common to perceive the colours with your inner eyes. You then use all of your senses to "see." I am sure that you have felt people radiate a special emotion, and if you don't know what that feeling is, your body starts to go through the colour-vibration-library and comes up with an answer based on the feel. A person in love usually has a light, pinkish feel about them, a dance you would like to join in with. Compare that with a person who is aggressive, and carries a denser, red energy and makes you feel that you don't want to dance around with them.

The aura is not only etheric. The field that is closest to the body anchors about one cm inside the skin, so that is how the etheric and the physical body are connected. Our inside will benefit from having a vibrant aura as well. Start by looking just outside the physical body. Search that little white shimmer that surrounds us all. Then continue to follow the edge of that shimmer when it turns into the next layer and so forth. If the person carries a lot of emotions around them, try to perceive where it is most intense. When you have found that place, what colour is most significant? Does it appear to be concentrated just at that place? It could be good to tell the person what you see. That emotion creates an imbalance that depletes the rest of their body, and that it could be a good idea to be aware of how the emotions seem to "rule" not only the mind but also the body.

If you have a pendulum, you can ask if the colour red is in the person's aura and then ask your body to feel into that, so you can start your own "colour-vibration-library" within. This is where you collect the data you get and will store information that you might need in the future. (Remember to air the library from time to time.) The next time you perceive the vibration of red while working with and on a person, your library will say, "Hey, red alert over here!" You will automatically have full access to all of the information you have collected. What to also pay attention to is the speed and intensity of the pendulum's swirls that will tell you how much of the colour the person holds in their field.

Also think about how you ask the question. Ask, "Do I carry the colour red in my aura as of Now?" rather than, "Do I carry the colour red in my aura?". The difference is the Now, because it is now that is of your interest.

Here are suggestions of a colour interpretation

Red

∂   You are warm, energetic and creative, holding a lot of sexual energy within you. I think of sexual energy as a Life Force. It doesn't have to mean that you are seeking a partner or walking around in lust all the time. Your life is governed by showing and being in very strong emotions.

Orange

∂   You have courage, carry happiness and sociability. It is a colour that shows that you have come to the realization of something important. You have changed your outlook on life.

Yellow

∂   This is the colour of mental activity. At the moment the intellectual is of great significance just now. Maybe you are preparing a lecture, or studying for an exam or just a little mentally tired.

Green

∂   You carry sensitivity, maturity, sympathy and calmness, showing that you have an open heart towards life and people and that you are trustworthy.

Turquoise

∂   You carry openness for speaking the truth from the heart. It may occur strongly in an aura if you are working with clearing "old patterns" and aiming toward a more vibrant life.

Blue

∂   Shades of blue in the aura mean peace and tranquillity. It can also show the ability or openness to clairvoyance and telepathy. Blue is the colour of the people who are loving, truth-loving and serious. Think of the blue suit that gives you a feeling of seriousness.

Indigo

∂   Indigo is blue in concentrate. Indigo in your aura can sometimes mean that you are a little lonely, there has simply been too much calm and serenity, maybe too much inner work. It also indicates that you have reached or carry a state of permanent inner stillness.

Purple

∂   Purple is the artist's favourite colour. It exists among people who refer to themselves as "seekers." The colour purple shows a sign of strong intuition and or concentration. Every time I look upon an artist performing, they have a lot of purple in their aura

White

∂ White in the aura often shows an awakening of creativity, and that you have reached a state of truth and purity within that also anchors you in your truth.

Black

∂ If black shows in the aura it can indicate that you want to hide something, or that you have been too purple for too long and you need some reflection time. If I feel that I am extra sensitive, I dress in black. It contains me and keeps me a little more in balance.

Grey

∂ Whenever I have seen grey shades in an aura that has indicated that the person is imbalanced and needs some support to feel the force of life within them.

WORKING WITH ANOTHER PERSON

The following exercises are powerful tools and should be done with much care for your partner.

AURA CLEANSING

1. Place your hands lightly upon the body 8or just above) and follow the flow of the body. Your intention is that you are cleansing any density that may reside in the auric field. Depending on the size and density of the body, you can do one, or both sides at the same time.
2. Start with the feet, move up through the knees and thighs, circle around the hip are / base chakra and make a slight stop at the navel chakra, move up through the solar plexus, heart, throat, up the head and make a circle just above the crown.
3. Then do same with the hands, moving up passing the elbow, armpit, circle around the shoulders, heart, rise up through the head.
4. Do the backside too.
5. End the whole cleanse by scanning the whole body, so all is released and in a flow. Then do a swirl around the head and connect the body o the spirit.

Tip! If you work with any healing tool this is a good flow to follow until you trust your intuition fully….

HOW TO MEASURE AND BALANCE THE AURIC FIELD

1. Centre yourself and connect to your pendulum and give it the picture and intention that the two of you shall now receive an indication how big your friend's aura is.
2. Ask the person to relax and centre themselves in their heart and body, and ask them to trust you.
3. Place yourself in front of the person about four meters away, and ask the pendulum to start to swirl in circles to indicate when you are in touch with the outskirts of their auric field. Approach the person slowly, with a steady hand and wait for the pendulum to start to move. When the movement starts, stop and let the pendulum work up a steady pace, then you can start to move around the person to see if there are any changes in the field, sometimes it is further away in the front of the body than the back.

This is also a nice way to balance an aura, if it shows a lot of different distances, ask the body what distance it feels comfortable in and ask the body and the pendulum to work together to balance the body.

HOW TO SCAN A BODY

1. Good to have pen and paper to write down your experience, during or just after. Give thanks to the person and the body that they give you the chance to work on them. Be in your heart centre and trust. Your intention should be to follow the leads you are given and be the observer. The person you will work upon can stand, sit or lie down. It depends on the cause of the scanning.
2. Become the person you are scanning. Breathe and relax into their body and their heart so they feel trust towards you and themselves, and allow yourself to be an open channel. Time has come for you to connect fully to the body and ask it to guide you towards any imbalances or anything else it cares to reveal.
3. Move your hands around the body with a slow, flowing movement, about 20 cm above, you are seeking to feel and perceive any changes in the energy field, like heat, cold, a wind, a sense of density etc. You can move your hands up and down. Often the density in the aura is placed a little everywhere. Just move slowly as too much movement can cause nausea.
   When you have a better feel and picture of the body you can move towards the seven energy centres. They are easy to feel and will provide information. Place your hands

above the point and feel. Write down what you perceive, even if it seems corny, it will make sense later on when you a have a fuller picture. It can be that you see a colour or a word. It is common to come in contact with an emotion or memory working on people. If any memory or emotion comes forth, think about, what does this emotion or memory mean to you? Is it a happy moment, sadness, or is it a feeling of curiosity. This is a time for honesty towards yourself to discover how much you can neutralize your own You. Write down this observation and make a note that it came from you.

4. When you have worked through the body, take a look, do you perceive any area on or around the body that seems to be imbalanced? If all looks and feels good, place your hands above the heart and connect with the intention that all is good, all is in balance, all is as it should be. To bring the person back into the body, use angel-feather light hands to brush over the body, starting at the feet, up the legs, tummy, shoulders, down the arms and hands, back up over the face and stroke the hair, then for a minute place your hands in stillness on the crown and again give thanks and say that you are now done.

TO RECEIVE A GIFT FROM YOUR HIGHER SELF

This is a little more advanced exercise, but fun.

1. Place yourself and your friend opposite each other and ask each other's Higher Selves if you can have access and move around comfortably in the other person's field.
2. Hold hands, breathe and find your comfort breathing in the same auric field with someone. Connect your hearts and take one more deep breath.

Each auric field surrounds the body about 1 – 3 meters. It is usually denser closer to the body and feels lighter further away. Your aim is that you shall visualize that you move into the other person's auric field all the way to the Spiritual body to collect a gift delivered by their Higher Self, and then you are to give it to them. Sometimes we don't perceive our Higher self and then we won't be able to receive gifts, as in messages and symbols etc. from them/us either. The colour range may vary from person to person so if the field does not hold these colours, just move on. It is, however, easier to have a starting point to guide you.

∂ Etheric body holds a light blue colour.
∂ Mental body holds a soft yellow colour.
∂ Astral body holds a pink colour.
∂ Causal body holds a blue colour.

∂ Soul body holds a golden colour.

∂ Spirit body holds a range of pastel colours.

1. Visualise that you take a step into each field of the person.

∂ Feel it, perceive if it's warm, cold, dense, feather light, strong, holds resistance, is open etc. It's good to write these observations down.

2. When you have reached the spirit body, you will receive a gift from the highest aspect of your friend. The way to deliver this gift through your body is to take a breath with the intention to send energy from your heart.

∂ Breathe in and feel that you hold the energy and "sense" the gift in your heart. Open your heart and direct it to the person's heart.

3. When the delivery is done, slowly withdraw your energy throughout all the six bodies until you sit in your own body and field.

4. Open your eyes and look into each other's eyes, give thanks to each other, take a breath and release your hands.

Tip! This is a powerful exercise, so take your time with each other. It takes courage to let someone into one's field and it can be a profound experience. A lot of emotions might be released and afterward you both might need to be in your own space for a while as well.

MEDITATION OF THE BLUE FLAME

Intention with this meditation is to release energies that no longer serve you

1. Imagine you are walking along a path. A bit ahead of you notice there is a fire burning with dancing blue flames. Walk towards the fire, place yourself beside it, breathe and connect to the fire through your heart. Feel the warmth and balance that is being created inside your core, you are safe.

2. Breathe and place yourself inside the fire, becoming one with the blue flames.
    Let the fire embrace you and when you feel that you and the fire are One, then let the blue flame heat and open all of your root-chakra, the energy of the colour and the flame begin to rotate and transform everything that no longer serves you, that is being held in your root.

3. After the flame has danced its dance allow your root chakra to expand to its former glory, trust that your body holds the knowledge of this and you can just relax.

4. Allow the flame to do the same in your other chakras.

Say thanks to yourself, for what you have learned from carrying this within, the knowledge it has brought you etc...

Do not let the process be dancing with your mind, trust that if there is anything that you need to know of what you are releasing, it will be presented to you in due time.

5. When the whole body has turned into One dancing expanded blue flame, let your flame burn out and find yourself sitting beside the fire again. Breathe and connect to your source both within and outside of you.

6. Exhale from your heart the colour that the body wants, let this colour spread throughout your body, to the sides, up and downwards.

7. Connect to your Source and find yourself sitting in what seems to be a cross (if you have a preferable geometric form please use this). Allow yourself just to sit and let the energies stream in through your root chakra, filling your whole body within and without until you are vibrating with pulsating energy. When done (trust that the body knows), it will return through the root chakra.

8. Take a breath, feel your feet placed balanced and steady on the ground. When finished, let a breath emerge from your heart, feel the bubbling new energy just fill you up, and let the body create the "space-you-need-for-today".

9. Take three breaths with the intention to return to Now, move your limbs, open your eyes, smile and just be…

BREATHING A WAY OF LIVING

I love breathing.
I love to know that I can revitalize myself so profoundly and so, so easily, and feel so good.

Once upon a time during a workshop, we were breathing a lot and it was exhausting to receive so much oxygen in combination with holding an intention and focusing solely on myself. I remembered that we worked a lot with the Unified chakra meditation. By the end of the weekend the teacher said that if we were to practice this meditation with its full intention, we would soon be able to take just ONE breath and unify ourselves, fully, from the core and out, from top to bottom. I thought, "Yeah, yeah, that will take time and effort. But being me and just starting on my path, I needed tools to keep me here Now and was reminded every time I attended the workshops. Once I was in need of a quick grounding during a dinner party and sneaked outside to breathe, and it worked. I was so happy to be able to take only one much focused inhalation with the aim to get myself fully together in a body I could handle until I got home.

I have also had the opportunity to use focused breathing in combination with releasing pain. I have breathed through pain waves and ended up being the one controlling and directing the pain wave instead of being the one that was tossed around in an ocean of just pain, with a feeling that there was no end to it.

I have inhaled energy downloads and felt how they have dissolved within, making me feel privileged. I have exhaled a lot of used up energy and felt the space it has held within me, knowing that I now can fill that space with something that revitalizes me.

I have hugged trees and stones and been able to connect to them through my heart-breath and been given the chance to breathe with them, a feeling mixed between humbleness and WOW!!!!! I have climbed heights within me performing fire breathing for 40 minutes, powerful…. I have also made myself sleepy performing long, deep breathings…

So if you haven't found the reason to dance with your own and Mother Nature's breath energy yet, you have a true life dance to look forward to.

LONG DEEP BREATHING

Deep breathing is the simplest form of breathing. It is the breath you had as a child. Unfortunately, most adults in our society have lost contact with deep breathing, often as a result of physical and emotional stress.

Remember: Breathe an equal amount of air in and out...

Benefits of deep breathing

If you can re-teach your body to breathe deeply, you will be affected in many ways. You will feel more relaxed and calm as you become more "alert." Your electromagnetic field (aura) becomes more vitalized and your immune system is boosted. Debris kept in your lungs will be gently removed, your blood will be purified and the increased oxygen to the brain and the body will support any form of healing of your mental and physical body. If you slow the breath below eight times per minute, the pituitary gland starts secreting fully. This will enhance your development of endurance, patience and relaxation. Breathe for a minimum of five minutes

How to breathe deeply

Relax your chest and shoulders and face. (The mouth is closed unless otherwise specified.)

Inhale, relax and expand your belly. Let it move outwards. The downward movement that is now created in the thoracic diaphragm makes the air naturally flows into the lungs to fill the vacuum just created.

When exhaling, allow your belly to sink deep towards your spine rather than trying to contract the chest. This creates pressure on the diaphragm and, as a result, the air will be squeezed out. Even when you think that you breathe very deeply, you can open up and release the breath even more. You can try this by lying on your back with one hand on your belly. Now you can easily feel the belly expand on inhalation and contract during exhalation.

SSSS-EXERCISE

This is a great exercise for when you feel stressed. It reduces the pressure on your diaphragm and gives your body a chance to relax and recover your energy quickly!

1. Sit comfortably with your spine and neck straight.
2. Inhale through your nose.
3. On exhalation, make the sound SSSSSSS until all the air seems to be out of your lungs.
4. Then do one sharp Ssss … to empty the air completely out of the lungs.
   Inhale and start the process again until you feel that you have created the outcome you want.

BREATHING EXERCISE FOR FOCUS AND GROUNDING

Lie down on your back in comfort, and place something under your knees if that brings you into a more relaxed state. Breathe and place your intention in your heart. Let the energy emerge from your heart and fill your entire body with sparkling light…

1. Inhale deeply and fill your entire stomach with air and let your tummy expand outward.
2. Hold your breath for as long as you can and keep your tummy expanded.
3. Exhale and pull your tummy back towards the navel area. Relax.
4. Imagine that in the outer part of your aura you see a pulsating white light. Inhale this transforming light into your body and when you exhale, direct the breath and imagine that it flows out of your feet.
5. Be in tune with your body and continue to breathe until your whole body and mind are relaxed and filled with sparkling lights…

Move your body, slowly open your eyes and with a deep breath come back to the room and sit up.

BREATH OF FIRE

I once did this for 40 minutes every morning and it was fantastic, and kept me in a good mood although a little floaty.

Breath of fire is not hyperventilation. Hyperventilation can occur if one is using the upper chest only and is losing control over the breathing. It could also happen if you are doing the exercise the opposite way. It cleanses the blood, the lungs and the cells. Expands the lung capacity as well as activates your "inner warmth" and increases oxygen delivery to the brain. It also keeps you calm and focused.
It is a fairly rapid technique with 2-3 breaths per second. Imagine the sound of a steam engine. It works like this: as you exhale, the air is being pushed out by the navel point and abdomen toward the spine. As you inhale, release the inward pull of the navel to allow the breath to automatically return to the lungs.

1. Sit on the floor in meditation pose or on your knees (or use a chair keeping your feet on the floor, if you have problems with your knees).
2. Keep your neck and spine straight, shoulders relaxed and keep your hands loose where you find it comfortable.
3. Breathe only with your nose.
4. Start by putting one hand on your tummy and breathe in. When you inhale let your tummy expand outward and when you exhale pull your tummy back.
5. Start by breathing faster than you usually do and keep your focus on the exhalation. Relax your tummy area and keep your spine straight.
6. If you lose your breath, go over and do some long deep breathing in between.

Tip! When you start working with this breath technique, start with 3 - 5 minutes and then work your way to 11 minutes or more.

ALTERNATE NOSTRIL BREATHING FOR BALANCE

1. Sit in comfort.

2. Keep your neck and spine straight and your legs crossed.
3. Relax your shoulders and keep a steady breath throughout the exercise.
4. Breathe only with your nose.
5. When you inhale let your tummy expand outward and when exhaling pull your tummy back towards the navel area.
6. Use your thumb and ring finger of the right hand. Use your ring finger to close the left nostril and inhale deeply through the right nostril.
7. At the completion of the inhalation, close the right nostril with the thumb and exhale through the left nostril.
8. Now inhale through the left nostril fully and deeply.
9. Then close the left nostril, exhale through the right, and repeat the pattern.
10. Breathe fully on both inhalation and exhalation.

I usually count my inhalations, so I am sure that both nostrils have breathed the same amount of times. You can also breathe in minutes. Start with five minutes and work yourself up to 15. Tip! For cooling down your body, breathe long and deep, through your left nostril after blocking off the right one. To energize yourself, breathe long and deep through your right nostril after blocking off the left one.

BREATHING THAT CLEARS YOUR BLOOD AND REVITALIZES YOU WITH FOUR SETS OF BREATHING TECNIQUES

1st round

∂ Sit comfortably with your legs crossed, back straight and neck stretched out.
∂ Keep your fingers in "gyan mudra": the tip of the thumb and the index finger touch each other making a circle. Relax your hands and place them on your knees or thighs.
∂ Close your eyes and put your attention on your third eye, the point between your eyebrows.
∂ Inhale and fire breathe for seven minutes.
∂ Inhale and hold your breath for 30 seconds.

2nd round

∂ Breathe long deep breaths through both nostrils. Continue for five minutes.
∂ Inhale and hold your breath for 15 seconds.

3rd round

∂   Breathe in through rounded lips and exhale through the nose. Continue for three minutes.

∂   Inhale and hold your breath shortly.

4th round

∂   Fire breathing for two minutes. Inhale and hold your breath as long as it feels comfortable.

Tip! Sit for a while and feel the energy being distributed around your body. If you feel there is any stagnation left, direct your breath towards that stagnation and breathe it free.

BREATHING & VISUALIZATION

1. Sit or lay down in comfort.
2. Breathe and find your pace. Let the breath light flow from your heart and merge with all of your bodies.
3. Breathe out white energy and let the energy fill up your body with the intention to expand your body.
4. Inhale and let your body expand throughout your auric field.
5. Exhale and relax. Stay in the size you have created.
6. Inhale and expand one meter outside the entrance door.
7. Exhale and relax, stay out there and open your ears. What do you hear?
8. Inhale and expand into the street. What do you hear? What do you smell?
9. Exhale and relax with your senses open and curious.
10. Inhale and expand into space. What do you sense?
11. Exhale and bring the feeling of space back into your body.
12. Inhale and listen to your own insides. Follow the blood streams and place yourself in the chambers of your heart.
13. Ask to be shown how your body looks from the inside.
14. Keep on breathing and just float around in your sensory system for a while.
15. When you are ready, keep an intentional breath so that you slowly bring yourself back to the now.

Move your body a little, open your eyes and before you start to do anything else, write down how you feel, what you experienced, etc…

mba

COLOUR BREATHING

I have always enjoyed working with colours
while breathing. My whole body starts
to vibrate deep, deep within and this mysterious smile comes on my lips. I am not sure what it is
all about, my body gets happy and then I will too…
I feel it is best to use the method of long deep breathing and then work towards breathing equal
amounts of air in and out...

Colour breathing is a powerful healing method, especially if it is done outside in nature.

Do not forget that the air transforms into energy inside your body, and the vibration and intensity of that energy is largely determined by your intention.

1. Sit in comfort. Breathe and place your intention in the core of your heart. Keep your spine perfectly straight in line with your neck. (If you bend your neck so you get a little double chin, you know that it is straight).
2. Let your breath emerge from your core and merge with the rest of the body, creating a bubble around your bodies that will expand and relax in tune with you.
3. Place the tip of your tongue on the top of your mouth just behind your front teeth. You then connect the two meridians going up your spine and down your front meeting in your perineum.
4. Breathe In slowly while counting to six through your nose. Hold your breath until you count to 12. Then breathe out slowly through your mouth while counting to six. Build up a slow, comfortable breathing rhythm.
5. As you continue to breathe, see and feel the air filled with a specific colour. Let it fill your entire body. See and feel the breath growing stronger and stronger. Visualize how it balances and creates harmony in your whole body.

To breathe colour for between five and 10 minutes can give a stunning effect.
If you are unsure of what colour you should use, breathe in the pure crystal white light. You can also picture the rainbow and let each colour pass through your chakras.
Do not forget: The colours have different qualities and produce different effects on your body and your senses. Here are some of the effects the colours will enhance you with.

Red breathing

Gives you energy and heat and strengthens your whole energy system. Helps with colds. Dries out your mucous membranes.

Pink breathing

Good for all skin problems and when you feel bloated. Soothes anger and the feeling of being alone. It can be used to balance up your emotions and give your mind worms a good shower.

Orange breathing

Balances your emotions. Heals muscle problems. Can also help with respiratory problems. Awakens your creativity. Restores the joy of life. An orange and pink combination (peach) is especially good for your muscles. A peach breathing is also good when we feel uncomfortable in any situation.

Yellow breathing

Relieves indigestion. Helps you to get access to your inner knowledge. The golden shade of yellow is an "all" healing colour, especially good when you have a mental issue

Green breathing

Relieves nervous problems. Awaken your sense of success in your mission. Light green breathing is good when you need to enhance your vision and release yourself from bad habits. It is soothing and has a cooling effect on your system.

Blue breathing

General reassuring. Facilitates your breathing. Wakes up your artistic talents. Is generally healing and good for children.

Indigo breathing

Increases healing. Helps to heal bones, especially the steel-blue colour, combined with a touch of green. Helps to open up your intuitive gift. It can have a strengthening effect on your energy system.

Turquoise breathing

Eases respiratory problems. Good for rheumatism. Can be combined with pink if you want to get away from the digestion problem. Opens up your communication skills, talking from your heart space…

Violet breathing

Helps your bones and nervous system. Purifying the body. Helps to detoxify your body. Wakes up your spirituality. The violet-breathing can help you to overcome the physical and mental imbalances in your energy systems.

Magenta breathing

Helps to detoxify your body. Good if you want to overcome strong, negative emotions and fixation. Most effective when combined with white. Can also help against infections.

A BALANCING BREATH TO HARMONISE THE BRAIN

In this breathe exercise you breathe with a left-sided focus.
Sit in comfort.

1. Inhale from your heart, exhale and push the breath from the left side of your body down to the base of your pelvis. Inhale and pull the breath up to your heart again. Repeat at least five times
2. Inhale from your heart. Exhale and push the breath up through your spine to the top of your crown. Exhale and bring it back to your heart. Repeat at least five times
3. Sit and feel the motion inside your head and body, relax.

THE CHAKRA SYSTEM-YOUR SEVEN ENERGY CENTRES

The word Chakra means wheel or the wheel of life and we have seven main chakras in our body. The chakras are like depots. I see these centres of powers as part of my body's library. They store knowledge, wisdom mixed with life force. With this knowledge integrated, I continue to walk on my path with greater awareness about myself. They may be depleted but never emptied. They are a constant part of my daily life, with me knowing or not knowing it. For each chakra I create balance in, I gain increased power and self-knowledge and feel that I can continue to walk on my path with greater awareness about myself.

Everything that lives pulsates with energy. We pulsate. We are a constant flow of vibrational energies, from the outer body into our smallest components in our cells. When we are stressed, sick or otherwise out of balance, our life force gets stuck and restricts the energies within. Our bodies no longer flow freely and will thereby affect every aspect of who we are and how we experience life. One can perceive the chakras as a kind of subtle energy centres for the exchange of energy between people and our surroundings. Another way to describe chakras is to say that they symbolize what and who we are, what we feel, how we feel and how we change. The theory and thoughts about us the humans having energy centres within our body exists in many cultures. The Bible speaks of the seven seals. The first Christians mention them as the seven churches. The Jewish Kabbalah uses the term the seven centres in the human soul. In medieval Europe the chakras were known in the alchemical tradition, related to metals and planets in a detailed system that came to be the basis of the alchemist. The number of major chakras varies slightly between different traditions. It talks about everything from five to nine major chakras. The most common number is seven.

The Chakras naturally strive for balance. The three lower chakras represents a more physical approach to life, and the top ones account for a more spiritual outlook and a higher consciousness. All chakras are equally important. Imbalance in one chakra affects the other as they all are intimately linked. The Chakras are each connected to the central nervous system via a stem which ends in the spinal cord. They also communicate with and affect the endocrine glandular system and therefore have a great influence on our psycho-physical well-being. They also have the ability to connect to our auric field and with this, they embrace our bodies as well.

Attached to each chakra there is said to be a certain gland, an organ, a defined element, a sense, a geometric symbol, different animal powers and a number. Each chakra also carries a specific colour. The West and the East of the globe and tradition describe the colours different. We in the western part of the globe describe them as the colours of the rainbow, with red in the root and purple in the crown. Even if "modern" science has not quite recognized the chakra system as something that actually exists, there are tests being performed that show that when measured energy, generated in the pelvic floor, rose up against the brain, the energy flow got held up at various points along the spine.

The chakras can be defined like this

1st Power is sprung from the family pattern you are born in, working towards resting in true independence.

2nd Power is born out of how you relate to others, working towards resting in a strong self-image.

3rd Power is born out of your personality, working towards resting in the feeling of being generous.

4th Power is sprung from your emotions, working towards resting in the feeling of confidence.

5th Power is born out of your will, working towards resting in the feeling of security.

6th Power is born out of your mind, working towards resting in the feeling of having an overview of your daily life and preferably into the future.

7th Power is sprung out of your "divine" connection (faith, religion, longing), working towards resting in being your own power sustained by your "divine source".

1 Independence

The emphasis in this centre is located in loyalty, identification and physical survival. You enhance your energy by valuing and protecting nature, your bloodlines (as in your ancestry) and how you view the bond you have with your family. You weaken your energy by holding on to negative family experiences (belief systems that you don't believe in any more) and feeling that your social and religious beliefs and values are better than those of others. The centre is located at the bottom of your pelvis and is linked with the organs you find around this area.

2 Strong self-image

The emphasis in this centre lies in control and relationships. Here you store the energy associated with sex, money, and relationships to people outside "your family." You enhance your energy by nurturing supportive relationships, letting go of sexual encounters that were not in balance, and working towards releasing any dependencies. You weaken your energy by trying to control other people, putting yourself in financial difficulty and hanging on to the memory of unresolved conflicts.

The centre is located just below your navel and is linked with the organs you find around this area.

3 Confidence

The emphasis in this centre is to cultivate your personal power. Here you find your sense of self-respect, honouring and valuing yourself. It also contains your ability to maintain personal boundaries. You enhance your energy by relying on your intuition, keeping your word both to yourself and others, as well as being true to yourself and your abilities. You weaken your energy when you break promises to yourself, manipulate others to gain their trust and when you are not able to keep personal boundaries. The centre is located between the navel and the ribcage and is linked with the organs you find around this area.

4 Generosity

The emphasis of this centre is emotions. To work from your "voice of heart" means to care for and to live in harmony, forgiveness and love for oneself. You enhance your energy by loving others unconditionally, when you allow them to experience the world in their own way. You weaken your energy by not allowing others to care for and love you unconditionally, and by allowing memories of old injustices to continue to control your life. The centre is located around your chest and is linked with the organs you find in this area.

5 Safety

The emphasis in this centre is will and choice, how you work your way out of old energy patterns and how you define your needs to the outside world. You enhance your energy by speaking truthfully, practicing self-control and letting others speak their truth. You weaken your energy by letting others tell you what you want and need, lying and being ashamed of what you think.
The centre is located in your throat area and is linked with the organs you find around this area.

6 Overview

The emphasis of this centre is intellect and reasoning. A closed mind limits you. An open mind gives you access. You enhance your energy when you follow your hunches, have an open mind to the world and possess the courage to take emotional risks. You weaken your energy by forcing through rational explanations, shutting your mind because you do not understand in the moment and by holding on to old grief. The centre is located between the eyebrows and is linked with the organs you find around this area.

7 Leadership

The emphasis in this centre is mysticism and grace, when your mind and your body feel in contact with something natural, but perhaps inexplicable. Someone prays and finds themselves in contact with their source. Another goes into the forest to get in touch with nature, while a third person finds stillness within themselves. There are many ways to reach one's own "grace." You enhance your energy by seeing your life from a higher perspective, where you allow yourself to ground in your silence, strive to maintain a strong self-esteem, and maintain connection with a higher energy source. You weaken your energy by living your life without faith, denying that you are led by a higher power other than your own mind, and by creating conditions for holding on to your spiritual development. The centre is situated in the middle of your head and is linked with the organs you find around this area.

BALANCING THE CHAKRAS BY USING TONING

Breathe, connect with your heart and when you feel in balance, move into the core of your heart. Focus on one chakra at a time and direct the energy towards that area on the body. Start toning using the mantra (word), focusing into that chakra, and continue until you feel the balancing is done. Working with another person, you can do this powerful connection. When breathing merge your inner heart with the other person's heart centre. Breathe until you feel that the two of you carry the same vibration.

LAM	Manipura - Root chakra
VAM	Swadhisthana - Navel chakra
RAM	Manipura – Solar Plexus chakra
YAM	Anahata - Heart chakra
HAM	Vishuddha - Throat chakra
OM (as a ringing bell)	Ajna - Third eye chakra
AOM	Sahasrara - Crown chakra as well as the entire body

HOOLA HOOPING THROUGH YOUR CHAKRAS

This is a great exercise to do every morning and night. In the morning preferably before you meet any other person and at night before you turn off your bed lamp. This exercise will balance you and create a good vibration within.

1. Imagine that you have a Hula-Hoop going straight through your chakras.
2. Put your intention on one chakra at a time and see the Hula-Hoop start swirling around in your chakra. It doesn't matter if it swirls clockwise or not. Let your body decide. It knows…
∂ Let yourself be transformed by the swirls and release whatever might be swung loose into a White fire. If during the day you feel a little unbalanced or have a loss of energy, take a minute and ask your body to swirl, breathe and just be…
∂ You might feel a little dizzy in the beginning and heat might be generated in your body, which is great if you are cold…

Tip: This is a great exercise to perform during a cleanse or any other focused transition in life.

EXERCISE & MANTRA SAT KRIYA AND SAT NAM

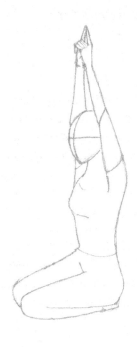

This exercise massages your inner organs, supports your heart and releases energy that has collected itself in the lower part of your body. According to Kundalini yoga this is like a yoga set all by itself. It cleanses out your entire chakra system by the fire you create while "pumping" the navel and chanting. Sat means "Truth" and Nam means "To Call." Together Sat Nam means "Truth is my identity," meaning that you call upon the truth that resides within you. Chanting repeatedly, you call this energy into your life, body, mind and heart.

1. Sit on your heels. If you find this difficult sit with your legs crossed. Hold your neck straight (the tip of your nose is pointing slightly downwards).

Hold your arms straight up, your elbows close to your ears. Your fingers are entwined with the first fingers pointing straight up. Keep your position straight. Be clear in your voice when chanting.

2. Chant the word SAT while pulling your belly button in towards your spine and inhaling. Imagine that your life force, Chi, Prana starts rising from your pelvis, your root chakra, up the spine throughout your crown chakra, your head.
3. Chant NAM while letting your belly relax and exhaling out.

This is the only movement you perform during the asana, in and out with your belly.
Time to conduct the Kriya is 3 to 11 minutes.
At the end take a few moments to feel how the energy moves around in your body, find your breath.

It is important that you rest the same amount of time as you have been active!
Be in comfort on your back, place a pillow under your knees, arms and hands are relaxing against the floor, connect to the floor. If you can do this exercise outdoors, connect to Gaia and let yourself be embraced by her.

BALANCE YOURSELF WITH QUICK AND EASY METHOD USING CRYSTAL ENERGY

This is an excellent way to start communicating with your body, your sensory systems and to become more "whole" in the aspect that all of you is aiming towards being One.
Say that you are in bodily distress!
First you need to create full contact with your physical body, your mind worms and your etheric bodies. Sit in comfort and breathe with the intention that shimmering light emerges from your heart. This light makes connections with all of your bodies and the result is a feeling of peace and clarity in combination with curiosity. Breathe and connect with your Higher Self and let yourself expand as much as you can, continuously filling yourself with the shimmering light.

1. Ask your body where the distress is located. Which chakra is involved? If there is more than one, be sharper in your intent and ask which one holds the core of the distress. Now when you have awareness of which chakra and body part is involved, this is how you proceed. Be focused, in a short period of time you will give yourself this gift.

2. Ask your body for the best suggestion to release the distress so you can be brought back into total balance. *Tell your bodies how long you intend to work this way, it can easily stretch out too long.*

3. Say out loud that you want to release the distress from your physical body in harmony and balance (no strong purges). There might be changes in your sleep and food intake that is normal.

   Why say it out loud? Then you engage your physical sensory system as well.

A. Choose a crystal that balances the chakra. Work intuitively with a pendulum for choosing a crystal, and then you can read about the abilities of the crystal. (If you don't know, choose a clear crystal.)

B. Place the crystal in a jar of spring water (make sure the glass is without any patterns) and large enough to support you with 10 glasses of water during this week. Keep the jar a day and night, preferably under the rays of the Sun and or the Moon.

C. When the water and the crystal have been merging, for a day or more, you are to take a glass of water each day, in the morning or at bedtime.

   You may want to add a little water in a small bottle as a carry-on for daily use if needed. If there is still water left you can add some alcohol to preserve it (50/50) for later use. Be sure that you remember what issue made you choose this crystal; it might be the same chakra but not the same issue you will encounter another time.

D. Choose an exercise that moves the body part you are working with. There are excellent movements to find and work with. It is best to do the exercise in the morning in combination with making the corresponding chakra sound.

E. Breathe through and expand the chakra. This is something you can do during the whole day. Make sure it is done before you start your morning and before you fall asleep at night.

F. When the week is over, meditate and scan your body with full awareness in truth towards yourself. Is there anything left? If so, how can you address this?

You will notice a difference very quickly…

BASIC CHAKRA BALANCING

This exercise you can do on yourself or on your friend.

1. Breathe, centre yourself in the core of your heart. When you feel balanced, let the energy merge out from your heart centre moving down into your palms.
2. Place both hands on or above the Heart chakra (if a woman is big chested maybe keep your hands above the chakra. You don't want to make the person uncomfortable) breathe and imagine that you sink into the energy, when you feel balanced continue.
3. Place one hand on or above the Solar Plexus, the other above the Throat chakra, breathe and imagine that you sink into the energy, when you feel balanced continue.
4. Place one hand on or above the Navel chakra, the other on or above the Third eye, breathe and imagine that you sink into the energy, when you feel balanced continue.
5. Place one hand above the base chakra, the other on or above the crown chakra, breathe and imagine that you sink into the energy, when you feel balanced continue.

Variation

1. Place both hands on or above the Heart chakra, breathe and imagine that you sink into the energy, when you feel balanced continue.
2. Keep one hand on the Heart chakra, the other hand is placed above or lightly on the Throat chakra, breathe and imagine that you sink into the energy, when you feel balanced continue.
3. Keep one hand on the Heart chakra, move the other to the Third eye, breathe and imagine that you sink into the energy, when you feel balanced continue.
4. Keep one hand on the Heart chakra, move the other to the Crown chakra, breathe and imagine that you sink into the energy, when you feel balanced continue.
5. Change hands on the Heart chakra.
6. Keep the "new" hand on the Heart chakra, the other on the Solar Plexus, breathe and imagine that you sink into the energy, when you feel balanced continue.
7. Keep the "new" hand on the Heart chakra, the other on the Navel chakra, breathe and imagine that you sink into the energy, when you feel balanced continue.
8. Keep the "new" hand on the Heart chakra, the other above the Base chakra, breathe and imagine that you sink into the energy, when you feel balanced continue.

9. Go back to holding both your hands on the Heart chakra, scan the body, does it feel balanced all over? If there is any part that seems to be unbalanced, just send a thought with balancing intention and breathe…

CHAKRA BALANCING BY RELEASING DEBRIS FROM THE AURIC FIELD

This exercise you can do on yourself or on your friend.

Self-exercise; easiest if you place yourself in front of a mirror or reflecting glass (so your silhouette shows). Check the auric field before you start, so you can see what has happened when you are done balancing.

1. Breathe, place yourself at the core of your own heart, feel how you merge with the energy, and then let it expand throughout all of your bodies.
2. Connect to the person's heart and ask their body to support you in balancing the chakras.
∂ It is best if the person sits on a stool, something without a back piece, or stands up, so you can work on both sides of the body simultaneously.
∂ Merge your heart energy with the person's heart energy. When you feel that you are dancing in the same vibration, start the balancing by placing one hand on or just above the crown chakra.
3. Second put your focus on the person's crown chakra. Move your hands up & down and "scan" the crown chakra, perceive how far the vibration moves around the body. Feel if there is any difference above and on both sides of the head?
4. Start the balancing by focusing and perceiving how the field around the crown and head vibrates in the same tone and visualizing that there is nothing stuck in the auric field.
5. Then continue throughout all the chakra points. Make sure you move your hands sideways to trace any imbalances between the back and the front of the body.
6. When you reach the Root Chakra, move your hands up and down between the chair and the floor.
7. When you have given yourself a "picture" of how the body and its chakras are doing, place one hand on the crown and one on the heart. Visualize a white light that dances from the crown and out through the root. If there is a feeling of adding colours to each chakra, to top them up, feel free to do that. Stay like this until you feel the flow is constant and powerful.
8. Afterwards you can re-check the field and the size of the aura. Are there any changes?

RAINBOW VISUALIZATION

This technique is good to do often, preferably every day. The intention is to strengthen and heal your entire system, both mentally and physically.

1. Sit in comfort, close your eyes and breathe. Breathe from the inner core of your heart and for every exhale let any stress you carry be released in the White transformative fire.
2. Visualize a Rainbow that goes in an arc above your head.
3. Visualize a ball in the red colour that comes out of the rainbow and bring this down through your crown chakra and into your body.
∂ Think and feel that it sends out a vibrant red spiral energy that reaches and heals all parts of your body. Concentrate on this vibrating energy. Let it spin down to your feet and feel how you swirl with it. See yourself wearing this Red! When the colour reaches and fills up your feet entirely, let the red colour disappear, absorbed by your body.
4. When the last of the red colour disappears into you, visualize an orange ball emerging from the rainbow above your head. Think and feel that it spins down through your body and fills you with its vibrant orange colour from your head down to your toes. When the last of the orange colour is absorbed by your body continue with the Yellow colour.
5. Let all the remaining colours of the rainbow - green, blue, indigo and purple fill and be absorbed by you. When the last of the purple colour is absorbed in your body. See yourself shining out of vitality and energy!
6. Then imagine that rainbow above your head starts to move downward towards you, until you are surrounded by it. *You are now One with this rainbow.* Each time you do this exercise the rainbow will grow stronger and stronger within you and around you. You will feel more vibrant, gain better health and contain a stable energy.

MERIDIANS

What is the Meridian System and the connection to Chi?

When I came in contact with meridians I found them such a source of intelligence. To be able to trace deficiencies within myself to the level of what this energy system provides is a gift. To have an instrument that I can connected with and be guided by when I have been building up my Chi by aiding my body and mind by better nutrients, sleep, exercises, it's a gift… To work with Meridian healing is a powerful tool. When you trace up and down an energy line to balance it, receive information, use your intuition and knowledge around the body and mind and be able to support with simple means.

I am very sensitive when it comes to acupuncture, I am easily over stimulated. Once I needed to release a muscle spasm and I told my osteopath that I was very, very sensitive, he didn't seems to understand the depths of my sensitivity, so yes my spasm went away and I turned into a raging bull. I worked at a bar that same night and was terrible to all of my costumers. My darling friend said "you need to get a grip on yourself, you are horrible…" Oops. I went for a walk, trying to calm all of this rage down and off course thought about what caused this state. I traced my day and realized that I had acupuncture. I looked at where the needle had been put. It was straight into my gallbladder meridian. I wondered if an overstimulation of this meridian could cause this emotional state of a raging bull. I did a healing and balanced myself and texted my therapist and told him he needed to de-activate me the following morning.

The Chinese has two names of life energy sources. "Lei" refers to what we eat, the nutrients flowing that spreads their energy through our blood system. The second is called "Chi," which is the universal life force that flows through what we call meridians. Meridians make up a circuitry or giant web that delivers Chi or life force energy to all of the organs and tissues of the body. This subtle energy system has been studied and treated in Traditional Chinese Medicine (TCM) for more than 5000 years. The ancient Chinese medical community identified 12 major meridian channels and eight extra meridian channels in the human body. Each of the 12 main meridians run along a particular route in the body and each is connected to the energy essence of the 12 major organs. Unlike the blood circulatory or nervous systems, the meridians running throughout the body are not visible to the human eye unaided by the appropriate technology. That's why it is called the subtle energy system. When we learn to calm, balance and stimulate these channels, we provide ourselves therefore with the energy flow we need in our daily lives.

Energy is a dynamic force. It flows in a continuous stream through our body. It is the basic layer for the body's solid and visible structures. Our body can be regarded as a battery, which needs to be re-charged. If this force decreases in our body, we usually get health problems. Every time you use your body or your mind, you lose Chi. Fatigue is a symptom that has a low Chi. When the Chi is completely gone we pass over. They have measured a person's weight in the moment of death and a weight loss of about two hectograms, which is said to be the weight of a body's Chi, its life force.

Chi circulates in your body over a 24-hour period. Each meridian and what it represents has its own two-hour maximum period of activity during this time, when it is active in cleansing and receiving Chi. Chi moves from one meridian (and the spirit of the organs it is connected too) to the other, and therefore always circulates the energy in your body.

Each meridian has a start and an end point. The end point is always linked to the starting point of another meridian. Therefore, always look at the nearby meridians if you discovered a lack of Chi in your meridian system.

Tip! If you have always had a lot of bladder infections, take a look at the meridians before and after the bladder meridian and see if strengthening these can support your bladder to be stronger. There are different ways of strengthening a meridian such as colon cleanse, drinking extra water, vitamins, acupuncture, movements, breath work, etc. Keep the intention steady on the task, whatever method you use.

Time	Meridian name
01.00-03.00 AM	Liver
03.00-05.00	Lungs
05.00-07.00	Large intestine
07.00-09.00	Stomach
09.00-11.00	Spleen
11.00-13.00 PM	Heart
13.00-15.00	Small intestine
15.00-17.00	Bladder
17.00-19.00	Kidney
19.00-21.00	Pericardium
21.00-23.00	Tripple warmer
23.00-01.00	Gallbladder

TO ENHANCE THE FLOW OF YOUR MERIDIANS IN A YIN YOGALIKE EXERCISE

Spend between 3 to 10 minutes on each exercise, so each posture will get your body into maximum benefit relaxation. Remember to always stay in the pose comfortably.

Lungs and Large intestine

Clasp your hands behind your back and slowly with your knees bent fall forward with great awareness. Straighten your arms over your head and towards the floor as far as you can in comfort. Breathe until you feel that you and the position are in balance.
Be careful when you come out of the pose

Spleen, Pancreas and Stomach

Sit on your knees. Place your feet by the sides of your knees and buttocks. Place your hands by your feet and slowly with great awareness move your upper body backwards, leaning on your arms. Stop when you feel that your knees are lifting from the floor. If you want to continue falling backwards to place your back on the floor, place pillows under your knees. When you are with your back on the floor, stretch your arms behind and above your head, grip your fingers together. Breathe until you feel that you and the position are in balance.

If you have difficulties to come into a full pose, you can take one leg at the time, keep your feet on the floor and knees up, while stretching your arms, you can also place a pillow under your knees so you keep your lower back in the floor

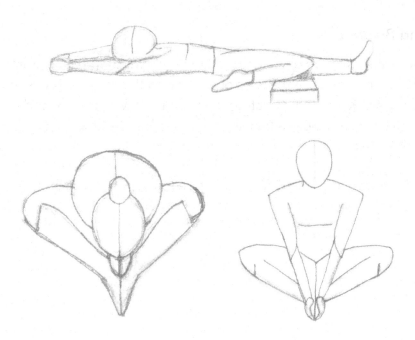

Heart and Small intestine

Sit on the floor and place your soles together. Grip your hands around your feet and pull the feet towards you as far into your crotch as possible. Try to reach the floor with your knees. Fall forward with great awareness and try to reach the floor with your nose. Breathe until you feel that you and the position are in balance. *You can place pillows under your knees, bend forward from your hips, be in comfort with your back.*
Alternative, use B if you have trouble bending forward

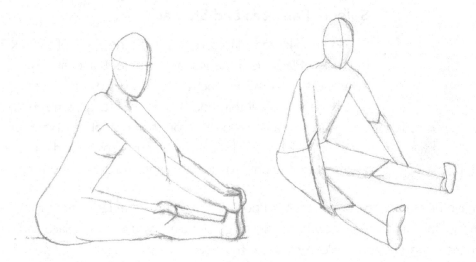

Kidneys and Bladder

Sit on the floor with both your legs outstretched. Lean forward with great awareness, bending from your hips, and try reaching the soles of your feet with both your hands. Aim your nose to touch your knees. Keep your legs straight if they are leaving the floor. Stop and breathe until you feel that you and the position are in balance. *Be careful with your neck, keep in line with the back if it's strained.*

If you have trouble leaning forward. Sit as in picture to the right, the importance is to stretch the backside of your legs.

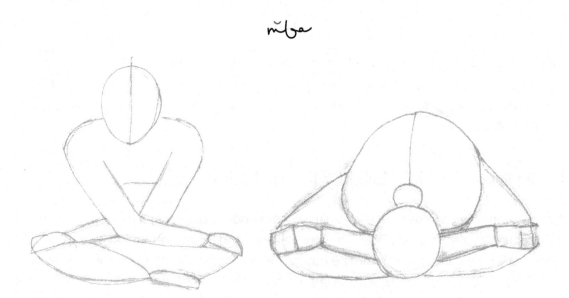

Triple Warmer

Sit with your legs and arms crossed, grab your knees and bend forward with great awareness aiming with your nose and touching the feet.

Be careful with your neck, keep in line with the back if it's strained. If you don't reach your toes, go as far as you can

Liver and Gallbladder

Sit on the floor with your legs straight and wide open. Try reaching your left foot with both your hands. Stay as long as you are in comfort and breathe. Repeat with your right leg. When both legs are done, place them together and fall forward. Breathe until you feel that you and the position are in balance. *Be careful with your neck, keep in line with the back if it's strained. If you don't reach our toes, go as far as you can.* If it is easier to bend one leg, use the right side posture instead

TO RELEASE BLOCKED ENERGY IN THE MERIDIANS

Working with Meridian release is to balance the meridian, by tracing any stops on the way and release that blockage. Use your intuition, be gentle and keep communicating to your body or the person you are working on. The reason for a stop can vary. It can be anything from a stuck emotion or a muscle that is too tight. Be open for all that comes to you.

Having ones meridians worked on can be a strong and powerful experience, since it is so much that gets stimulated within your physical body as well as your etheric bodies. Therefore, you need to go slowly and have all your senses alert to what is happening.

Example: If there is a stop all along the meridian of the large intestine, could that mean the body is constipated? Ask how the bowel movements are. (Do you or your client go everyday to the bathroom, doing number two?) If so, could the blockage be more of an emotional one? Maybe you or your client is stressed and never feel that there is time to just be. I believe that you can trace the meridian outside the physical body, they reach into the auric field. Remember the auric rings, it can be an idea to ask if they are meridian related.

1. Starting the healing by massaging the feet and hands of the person is a good way to create a flow, since the meridians begin or end in the hands or feet. It is also a nice way to calm the person's mind and let them get used to your energy.
2. Put your hand on the meridian starting point. You can either visualize that the energy flow goes from the starting point on the meridian to the end point or use your fingers and trace along the line with feathery fingers. There is a point of being more physical in this method, it is easier to discover imbalances when you are using a feathery touch on the body, you can detect little "shivers", hot or cold flashes etc.

THE FIVE ELEMENTS HEALING, USING A CRYSTAL

When you feel that you have gained some experience in working and tracing along the lines. You can start using a pendulum or a crystal to receive a little extra information, going a little more etheric. The crystal you choose as your tool shall be very in tune with what work you are expecting from it and has to carry great sensitivity.

Using this method you will bring balance to the whole body quicker (you are working on 5 meridians instead of 12). These organs hold a lot of vitality and by creating a flow within them: a balanced energy will flow out into the rest of the bodies and organs.

Spring - Liver
Summer - Stomach
High summer - Heart
Autumn - Lungs
Winter - Kidneys

Working on yourself;

Have the meridians drawn up on a piece of paper; this will represent your body. The more in tune you are, the more you will perceive in your body

1. Start by intentionally opening up the throat and the lymph nodes, ask for them to flow. If there is a lot of congestion in this area, conduct a light massage over the area.
∂ Massage the hands and feet gently, with the intention to open the flow
2. Check the start and end points of the meridians, you can use a pendulum to ask, perceive if they are blocked. *Here you work with your "paper body".*
3. Trace along the first line, how does it feel? Notice everything that comes to mind?
4. Place the crystal on the end point of the meridian
5. Place your hand on the start point and by intention, move the energy downwards on the meridian, towards the end, and at the same time you pull out the energy with the crystal into the white fire.

Working on others;

1. Start by intentionally opening up the throat and the lymph nodes, ask for it to flow. If there is a lot of congestion in this area, conduct a light massage over the area. Massage the hands and feet gently, with the intention to open of the flow
2. Check the start and end points of the meridians, you can use a pendulum to ask, perceive if they are blocked.
3. Trace along the first line, how does it feel? Notice everything that comes to mind?
4. Place the crystal on the end point of the meridian

5. Place your hand on the start point and by intention, move the energy downwards following on the meridian, towards the end, and at the same time you pull out the energy with the crystal into the white fire.

Continue until you find that there is a constant flow in the meridians and the body feels balanced. End by just stroking with feathery hands and fingers over the body so it returns like being caressed by a gentle breeze, so it returns gently and peace-filled.

CHAPTER 5

HEALING

There are many books about healing, so I would like to present what I feel is a basic "touch" and if this resonates with you, there's a world out there with wisdom, knowledge and methods to explore and learn from.

TAKE GOOD CARE OF YOURSELF AND THE ENERGY YOU CREATE

When I talk about energy, it is my belief that we all hold our own power, our own ability to heal, our own endurance and strength, to be able to live a daily life in balance on our physical, mental and energetic levels.

Our body reworks most of what it is supplied with, to energy. If you live a balanced life where you sleep enough, eat nutritious food and make sure that the body's muscles, organs and skin are being in motion, you will feel good and in balance. If you are not in a good balance you will take from your body's energy resource and begin a slow but steady depletion of yourself. Even if we do our best to follow the above advice, a constant input of physical and emotional stress will empty our energy resources. The trick for a balanced life with yourself is not to lose more energy than you bring in.

The different types of thoughts and actions that direct energy around the body, providing them with vital information is often not grounded in your own truth. There are many other ways to walk one's path than the habitual ones. What works for your mother, friend, and partner might not work for you. One way to find out is to increase the awareness of yourself, your resources, and review and fully accept your needs to keep a flourishing day.

Imagine this about your daily energy resource.

∂   You have 100 light bulbs in front of you. These represent your daily energy resource. Your sleep was disturbed, and when you wake up 90 bulbs of 100 are lit.

∂   You overslept, so you got to rush to work without breakfast, it cost you an additional 10 bulbs. Rushing in at your office you discover that your computer is broken so you have no time to prepare for the meeting you had planned and you get even more stressed out, now you're down to 60 bulbs and the day has just begun...

What do you usually do?

You are short 40 light bulbs and have no control over the daily events...

- ∂ Drink coffee with lots of sugar?
- ∂ Pour yourself an energy drink?
- ∂ Enter the storage room and kick a wall?
- ∂ Bite the heads off of your colleagues?

The above actions are borrowed energy resources and will not be able to turn on some of your lights, but will instead cause more lights go out…

What could you have done to ease up this daily chaos?

Call your work and ask a colleague to help you bring forth the material for your presentation, so you have time to have some breakfast (since everyone at work knows that you need to keep your blood sugar steady to be at your best). Take responsibility for coming late to work, in front of your boss (even if it was not your fault that the bus was delayed). On the way to work, you could have listened to music that you know will make you calm and focused, instead of up-tempo music that you listen to when you want to be active.

Tip: Keep an interest and awareness about your body. Communicate with it, your body holds the information you need and will gladly guide you forward. Figure out what you think is fun to do. Move towards actions that provide you with energy and the feeling of expansion. Decide that you want to understand where your energy is being dispersed during a day. By knowing this you can increase or minimize your flow during the day, accordingly to your needs. Do not let anyone else determine over your energy resources. Decide that the energy you release during a day you also bring back (by walks in the nature for instance).

ABOUT HEALING YOURSELF

When life feels cluttered, if there is chaos or you do not understand what is happening around you, always seek the underlying causes. This can be done in several ways. Here I present some suggestions.

Breathing with intention using the Unified Chakra breath

An aid in any situation no matter what the case is would be the Unified Chakra breath
It takes some practice, more so to re-program your physical body to merge with the whole of You in just One breath. *This is my own Quick fix when I need time out to regroup my Me and refocus….*

I breathe in Light, through the center of my Heart
I ask my physical body to expand light from the center of my heart
I let the light expand throughout my whole body including all of my etheric bodies

I breathe in Light, through the center of my Heart
I let the light connect Me with My source both above and below to give me clarity and balance

I breathe in Light, through the center of my Heart
I AM in unity of my my Spirit

As a standard task every morning, create your light channel to have a steady flow of light within you. As soon as you are feeling stressed, out of balance, or when you need to stay focused and concentrated and so on, take a breather. It will take some time to re-program your body and mind, but by being consistent and doing the breath many times with the accurate intention you will very quickly reach the point where One breath, one inhalation is all that is needed to compose yourself.

Meditate

Place yourself somewhere where you can sit undisturbed, in comfort and relaxed.
Ask about clarity in the situation you want to address. When you meditate, have all your sensory systems open wide. Keep faith in what comes to you. It is your own inner

knowledge that comes forth. The more precise you are in your intention, the clearer images and phrases you will receive back as answer. Do not be surprised if you get symbols in the form of animals, tones, colours, etc. Do not discard what comes to you, even if it seems incomprehensible or too simple. Sooner or later you will understand what the message was.

Reflections

Another important tool is the reflections of our surroundings. Reflect on the following statements;

- ∂ What I give out, I also receive.
- ∂ What I surround myself with creates my situation at the moment.
- ∂ Am I met by acidic, complicated people or by happy, helpful ones?
- ∂ Am I respected by those I meet or not?
- ∂ Will this reflect back my own self respect?
- ∂ If I think positive and uplifting thoughts about myself and others, will I receive the same energy back?

Daily life symbolisms

We don't only get symbols in our dreams and meditations. We are surrounded by a very rich living symbolism in our daily life too. It is so close that we often do not give it enough value and attention. Is it messy in my life?
How does my apartment look?
Start by cleaning up and I can assure you that you will hold a clearer mindset when you are done.

The Body

Sometimes you can make very tangible parallels. For example, if we look at our own body we can find a great deal of symbolism; Do I squeeze my body's energy flow by wearing clothes that fit too tight? What is it that I want to hold onto so tightly? Am I afraid that my Me will leak out and show my true nature to the world? If we start having problems with our eyes - is there anything in our life situation that we want or think we need to cover up?
It is often said that our left half of the body is the feminine and the right our male. *If I perceive an imbalance between these two sides, maybe there I have an imbalance in my relationship*

towards women, or can it be that I don't dare to flourish my very own feminine side? This is oversimplified, but worth giving a thought.

Dream and Meditation diary

Even insignificant dreams usually have something to tell us. Do not forget your dreams, they can tell you more than you think (how to interpret dreams see chapter; How to develop your awareness).

Action

Now that you know the cause of your situation, you can proceed in several ways.

∂ Light your white fire. (chapter; How to develop your awareness)
∂ Give yourself healing.
∂ Scan and breathe through your body and release what feels uncomfortable.
∂ Place yourself in a meditative state and focus on releasing whatever seems to be stuck.
∂ It can also be effective to make a simple affirmation. See page

To affirm is to take active responsibility for what your reality looks like. All our thoughts consist of energy. Everything we think is in orbit around us, affecting us and perceived by others, more or less consciously. If I want to change my situation? I change my mind! An affirmation is in the present tense. You create your reality here and now.

MY BODY FEELS CONGESTED AND NEEDS A RELEASE

Remember that the flow follows the thought. What is it that you want to accomplish? The more focus your intention has, the better result you will receive. These are excellent tools to use on yourself, especially when you are seeking an answer to an issue. Feel where the stagnant areas are located, rake and sieve the area, let your body decide for how long it is needed. During the healing, meditate on the issue and be certain that you will get the answer, it might come as a picture, a memory, a feeling, be open and receive.

The Sieve

This is a splendid method if you feel that "something" is really stuck in the body.

The method releases the etheric energy that is stuck in the physical body. Imagine that you take your sieve and drag/pull it through your foot and continue up your leg. If you feel any resistance that is really stuck and it is hard to get through, increase the size of the sieve-holes to make it easier to sieve through and to get into a flow. And then when you feel less resistance you can decrease the holes again. Continue and work through the whole body or concentrate on specific parts of your body. You can also sieve another person's body or an item as well as a plant or a room. The limit lies within your imagination.

The Rake

Sometimes when a muscle is stiff or when you feel that the pain of the body is rooted inside the pelvis or any other place that is hard to get to, use the rake! Imagine that your hand/hands transform into a rake with beams of light that go out from your fingers.

Imagine that you rake the area that feels stuck. The light beam goes the whole way through the body and out on the other side. You will feel how the energy releases and starts to flow. If you have the feeling that there is an organ that needs healing, rake through with great care and when you feel the energy flowing then you can start to balance the organ by filling it up with light. When you finish working it is nice to rake the whole body through. You can also rake your aura. Feel free to follow your mind and do what needs to be done.

These are very powerful tools. If you give hands-on healing or similar sessions and it feels like you want to "push" for release, before you do, try these two methods to release the energy on a more subtle and deeper level.

DISTANCE AND SELF HEALING USING YOUR KNEES

Distance healing is a method where you can heal yourself and others of past moments, the present and the future. Your recipients can be persons, animals, objects and land anything that contains the force a Life. All have a vibration of Life within them. If you work on a person or an animal, it is easy to use the Knee method. If you are not the "object" of attention make sure that you have informed the recipient so they are prepared and can contribute with their full awareness. Make sure you have their permission to work. If there is any slight feeling of a, "No, do not start," maybe contact the "object" of your attention and make sure that all is clear for the healing. Before you start make sure that your intention is clear. Make sure that you feel in tune with the person or animal before you start. A suggestion is to have pen and paper nearby so you can take notes during the session.

1. Sit in comfort. Take a moment to breathe and find stillness within. Set your intention.
2. Let light emerge from your heart centre onto your palms until you sense there is a nonstop flow between the heart and your palms. Then the time has come to focus on your task.
3. After you are finished take a moment and just sit in ease and let the entire light dance in and out through you. Feel if there is anywhere that needs more attention, if so direct some extra light towards that area.
4. When done, if possible, lie down on your back, breathe through the body and centre yourself in your heart. Return to the present moment.

Self healing using your knees

You can use your knee as a tool for this method or choose to put your hands where your intuition tells you. This method can be used wherever you are, when you sit on the train, the bus, or simply at home (this is a good method to use for distant healing too).

∂   The backside of the lower part of your leg represents the back of your body whilst the front side represents the front of your body.

∂   Let the knee cap represents your head and also the crown chakra.

∂   To distinguish your six other chakras you can first place your hands just under each other from the cap to the foot, which will give you a feeling of what part of the body/chakras you are working on. You can grip the whole leg around and then work on both the front and back sides of the body, or you can work each side separately.

∂   You can also decide that one leg stands for the front side and the other the back side, what flows best in the moment.

1. Sit in comfort and make sure you have your knee available to reach all over. To sit on a cushion placing one knee pointing upwards is easiest.
2. Take a moment, breathe, find stillness within, let light emerge from your heart centre to your palms until you feel there is a nonstop flow between these and then focus on your task.

3. Place your hands on the kneecap and let the flow of light fill you until it "says" it is done.
4. Work downwards until you reach your foot and then make a connection with the earth or root chakra.
5. Change legs and repeat the process.
6. After you are done take a moment and just sit in ease and let all of the light dance in and out through you. Feel if there is anywhere that needs more attention and send some extra light towards that point.
7. When done, if possible, lay down on your back, breathe through the body and centre yourself in your heart and return to the present moment.

HEALING CRISIS

After undergoing treatment, many people report an increased tempo in their lives.
Suddenly, there are so many more things to take care of, so many more loose ends that seem to flap around, uncontrolled. In addition, many individuals have stated that several difficulties arise. Negative emotions emerge, often coming from the distant past, or even people they have known long ago pop up in their lives again, like old best friends, boyfriends/girlfriends, people you thought that you had dealt with, that still
seemed to have unfinished business with you. Some also exhibit physical problems such as headaches, upset tummy and colds. These symptoms of stress mentioned above are only an indication that a healing has worked deeply, and can be called a healing crisis. When you are open and able to receive deep healing it will affect your life on a much deeper level than just the physical issue for which you sought support. This is because many parts of a person's life are affected by the specific problem that was to be healed. When a particular area begins to heal, that motion starts a big "reshuffle" in the body and mind, which means that energies flow in their "truthful" ways. It can be increased flows in certain areas and decreased flows in others.

For example, if you have financial issues, the problem might not just be to get a new well paid job. There are usually deeper causes that can be linked to a sense of responsibility, discipline, learning, culture, etc. When the economic problems begin to heal or clear up, it will affect all of these areas too. Patterns and emotions will give way for new insights and ideas. Maybe you will move to a less expensive house to be able to become a gardener, and in doing so fulfil a long-lived dream of yours. Whenever there are changes, good as well as bad, there is a period of adjustment so that the parts of life that have been affected can become accustomed to this new way of living one's life. A healing crisis can be compared to replacing the furniture. During the move mostly everything tends to look messy, worn out, even ugly. Dirt and dust show up. But after a thorough cleaning and with the new furniture in place, the room looks better than ever before. It is the same with personal healing. It may seem confusing and uncomfortable before the healing is complete. When everything is quiet again, you see the important progress that has taken place. You will feel better and your life will be healthier. So do not be afraid if you are affected by the described crisis. It is just a sign that proper healing occurred and your life will soon appear brighter and filled with joy. Just continue to care for yourself, release all negative emotions into a transformative white fire and allow your healing to work.

Tip: You will never receive more to handle than you and your body can support.

TO CREATE AND RESTORE THE BALANCE WITHIN; ON A PHYSICAL, EMOTIONAL AND SPIRITUAL LEVEL

Sometimes we need to just re-calibrate ourselves

I have found this a good exercise to do.
Lie comfortably on moderately hard ground, wear loose clothes so that you feel at ease and can breathe freely. Close your eyes and turn your awareness inwards, at the same time become aware of all your senses and feel into;
How you feel? How does your body feel? Feel the weight of your body against the ground. How does it feel? Sense your spine, stomach, head, shoulders (continue). What is your body telling you? Let your thoughts come and go in an easy flow. Do not stop them…

1. Feel a golden light in your heart.
2. Slowly, let it expand by filling your body up piece-by-piece, right down to the soles of your feet and to the top of your head.
3. As the light fills your body, feel yourself relaxing more and more. Let the light lift off any fatigue or burdens you carry and fill this space with your life force. Once your entire body has been filled with light, rest in it for a moment and sense the difference from when you started.
4. Then allow the golden light to merge with your cells and fill up every cell with the light, rest in this state for a few moments.

5. You have now released energies that you no longer need to carry within you. They are now lingering around your body and need to be cared for. Give them a colour.
6. Continue to let the light spread outwards and create a bubble around your body.
7. Visualize that this bubble is magnetic and will pull these coloured released energies towards the bubble's wall. When you feel, see or sense that the wall is filled with the colour, take some more deep breaths so everything is released, breathe out from the core of your body and out.
8. Last, direct the coloured bubble towards the White fire to be transformed.
9. As you did in the beginning, allow the golden light to merge with your cells and fill up every cell with the light. Rest in this state for a few moments and slowly bring yourself back. Close your eyes and turn your awareness inwards. Become aware of all your senses. Ask yourself;

∂ How do you feel - how does your body feel?
∂ Feel the weight of your body against the ground. How does it feel?
∂ Sense your spine, stomach, head, shoulders (continue).
∂ What is your body telling you? Let your thoughts come and go in an easy flow, do not stop them…
∂ Is there anything else that needs to be embraced? Ask your body. Trust what comes to you.
∂ Send this feeling out towards the White Fire and let it be transformed. When you feel that you are in balance feel the golden light embracing the whole of you, now that you can walk in your own beauty.

INCREASE OF FREQUENCY

When you start to work with energy, healing, personal awareness on different levels, you will start to receive what is commonly known as a frequency increase. The feelings of the increase are discomfort at the beginning, you will however learn how to dance with it and make it your friend.

Most common symptoms are that seem like you have migraine, the flu, tummy problems, and dizziness, loss of appetite or an increasingly craving for sugar, salt, fat, or comfort food. It is not unusual that after you have been attending a workshop, where your body and mind has undergone deep relaxation etc, that you get the blues. If you go to the doctors, they seldom find any reason for your discomfort and even less a cure. You will find that the days vary. Some days the process is "unbearably" intense, and other days all is good, and you might feel that all your symptoms and feelings are hanging outside of you like a coat, for everyone to witness. There is no coat, very often other people don't even notice any difference in you, it's all internal. The process is very intense and it is important to feel into your body and mind. If you have a feeling that you need to rest, rest!

Feel into if you need more nutrition or your body may want to stop eating meat, if you are a meat lover, do not panic, it might just be a period of your life. Maybe it means more that your body prefers to eat organic meat and not processed meat. Nature is a great act of balance for your entire system. Walk it off. Hug some trees. Rinse your head in a lake. Pick berries and eat them with grace. Lean your back against a tree and just sink into the root system and travel for a bit...

Tip! Take the "clear-headed" days as an opportunity to enjoy and feel and do normal stuff. Working towards being here and now, will absolutely help the process.

Energy boosting

I will mention some of the symptoms that might occur when receiving high dosage of energy boosting;

- ∂   Strong attacks of drowsiness or extreme sleepiness
- ∂   Sudden bursts of extreme high energy
- ∂   Waking up feeling "lost", not sure where you are or who you are
- ∂   Very high pitched tones in your ears or the complete opposite, like you have a bumble-bee in your ears
- ∂   Extreme thirst or realising that you are dehydrated (electrolytes can be a good quick fix)
- ∂   Your body temperature is either high or low (no, you are not in menopause or having a fever)
- ∂   Strong body odours
- ∂   Greasy skin and a feeling of wanted to "scrub-down-yourself"
- ∂   Getting a feeling of vertigo, even if you are walking a ordinary street
- ∂   Suddenly you are very sensitive and cannot be around your normal friends, or in places you usually visit, a little like social phobia
- ∂   Wanting to change occupation, from one day to another or any other strong feel of change
- ∂   Getting a deep feeling within about wanting to merge with your "source"

The list can go on forever, just be aware that changes will occur and that your body, mind, soul are dancing with your Higher self and that your dancing is a little rusty...

MEDITATION THE BUBBLE OF HARMONY

This meditation holds the intention of embracing yourself with a bubble of your own light to feel more in comfort during your day or night...

Sometimes there seems to be a need to understand how sensitive One is. It can be that you have trouble keeping your own strength at work. You seem to become tired as soon as the first coffee break is over and you have chatted with your colleagues. You are ready to head home…

When starting to walk one's path and becoming more aware of how one is interacting with the world around, you are bound to develop a stronger sensitivity and that can be a of nuisance sometimes…

I have several times received an unpleasant vibe from close ones, saying "Ahhh, YOU ARE SO SENSITIVE THESE DAYS", and "I feel that I can't say or do anything without getting such a strong reaction from you" etc, etc. I think it is hard enough choosing a different way to look upon oneself and changing how one interacts without this extra interference,(changed a little, make sure it's clear for you) This little bubble of light has always been a great support…

1. Place yourself in comfort
2. Breathe and centre yourself and focus your intention to the core of your heart and connect to your source.
3. From this core let a colour emerge and start to blend with the rest of your body in the shape of a bubble that is covered in the White fire as an aid for transformation
4. Imagine that the bubble will support you to filter out all that does not resonate with you Now.
∂ The bubble keeps your energy vibration intact and will only let you dance with vibration that resonates with you
5. Imagine that energies that may disturb you will bounce back to the sender or be transformed by the white fire that covers the outside of the bubble
∂ Inside the bubble you are in total balance and harmony
∂ Remove the bubble when you no longer need it and practice being in balance and harmony as often as you can without the support of the bubble

Surrounding oneself with a supportive shield will keep you more aware of when and sometimes to whom you lose your strength. By keeping an open heart and letting the heart tell your mind why this occurs you can in time strengthen yourself towards limiting and preventing any leakage you are allowing…

CHAPTER 6

MEDITATION

MEDITATION

For me, the meaning of a meditation is that "I have created", by using a method to "still my mind" and that I have "re-programmed" my body to remember signals, such as a special breathing technique or a particular sound. My body knows, for instance, the "calming down" breath and can differentiate this one from the "get some action" breath. The better you can use visualization while having a focused intention, the quicker you will reach your desired result!

In this chapter you will be presented with many different kinds of meditations. They are meant to be inspirations for you. If you feel that the tea cup becomes a coffee cup, go for that, it's not the tea that is the focus, it's the stillness of what comes with just sitting and sipping that is the point. Even if your level of experience varies, you can always read through and get some benefit from the more advanced meditations (make it your own).

Breathing

Breathing, for me is essential in a meditation. Make it a habit to always breathe in and out through your nose. It will keep you from getting a dry throat. In addition, the nose works as a purification filter. Let your stomach expand on inhalation so that the lungs get filled to their maximum air capacity (imagine that they get filled down to their very bottom) and then let your stomach be pulled back towards the spine to empty the lungs completely. This will allow your diaphragm to relax (a muscle that wraps around and under the ribs), and let your lungs receive more oxygen and your body will be re-vitalized

You can also practice focused breathing. Visualize, as you exhale, to direct the air to a different path, such as out of the arm instead of the nose. For instance, say that your arms are tired after working in the garden. To realize stagnant energy in them try this

∂ Breathe in fresh energy, direct the exhalation out through your arms and "see" how the stagnated energy exits and transforms, leaving you with less heavy arms. You can add some sparkles that will make the feeling stay on.

∂   Breathe through your entire body in this way. With focused intention and visualization in combination with focused breath, you create a strong programming for relaxing and transforming your body.

BENEFITS OF MEDITATION

The brain waves of meditators show they are healthier. It is said that meditators shift their brain activity to different areas of the cortex, for example brain waves in the stress-prone right frontal cortex move to the calmer left frontal cortex. This mental shift decreases the negative effects of stress, depression and anxiety. There is also less activity in the amygdale, where the brain processes fear.

Health Benefits

Numerous studies have shown that meditation has health benefits, generally related to the decrease in stress that occurs through meditation.

Control Your Own Thoughts

Most people are victims of their own thoughts, and have no means to control what goes on in their minds. I find that regular meditation leads to the ability to control my thoughts, and even the ability to stop them completely. This creates peace of mind and enables me to achieve what I need to do.

Detachment

When our minds are in control, certain things, even little things annoy and irritate us. The only effective solution is to develop detachment and keep things in perspective. A powerful benefit of meditation is that it helps us to gain a broader perspective and detach ourselves from what is insignificant so that we experience equanimity under any circumstance.

Happiness and Peace of Mind

Meditation offers peace of mind and takes us to the source of happiness. If our minds are all over the place then we are constantly being attacked by limited patterns of thinking. If we can meditate with a still mind, we will discover a deep and peaceful happiness.

Meditation helps people to build concentration. Whether through work, sport or music, concentration is essential to achieve our best. When we are able to focus on one thing at a time, we become far more powerful, and our energy does not have to cut through many different layers of thinking and distraction.

Spontaneity and Creativity

When we live in the thinking mind,
we are usually preoccupied with the past or future. If we can learn to silence the mind, we can realize that anything is possible, and our creativity and spontaneity in life can come alive.

Discovering Your Life Purpose

Many people feel that there is something missing. They may have relationships, children, a good job etc, and still something feels missing. Usually we look for meaning in life in the outside world. However, everything we need is right here inside. In meditation we gain a new perspective of life, without being filtered through our ego. Meditation can become a lifelong process of answering the eternal question: "Who am I?"

BASIC MEDITATION

This is a meditation that will bring you and your body into a thorough relaxed state. Using your intention, see, feel and be with your body during the whole exercise. The thought is that when you INHALE you expand your tummy, your etheric body, your whole you, and when you EXHALE you relax fully on all levels.

Tip: Mind follows Intention...

1. Inhale and Exhale. Focus is to be here Now, find your heart centre find your breathing, keep both feet on the floor, sit in comfort, and keep your eyes closed.
2. INHALE - Move your focus and intention to your feet and feel your feet expand as much as possible, like floating out on the floor. *Keep your breath in as long as possible.*
3. EXHALE, relax and feel your connection to the floor.
4. Move your focus and intention and keep on breathing as described, always feel connection to floor with your feet.
5. Continue with your;

∂ Knees
∂ Hips and Pelvis
∂ The Whole Legs (from top to bottom)
∂ Tummy and Torso
∂ Chest and Heart
∂ Shoulders, Arms, Hands and Fingers
∂ Throat
∂ Face
∂ Inhale and exhale through each hair on your head

6. INHALE through your whole body, expand as much as possible, *hold your breath as long as possible*, feel how you expand.
7. EXHALE through your whole body and relax fully…..

MEDITATION TO CREATE GOOD FLOW DURING THE DAY

The intention is to create a flow of steadiness…

1. Sit down, take a few deep breaths and relax with every exhalation.
2. Light the White transformative fire as a support during the meditation.
3. Let an energy emerge from your heart and surround your whole body, this is your own inner light. You are safe and in balance…
4. Focus your mind on the day that lies ahead of you (or any situation you wish to create a good inflow and imagine a clear light surging through the whole day, like a river.
5. Imagine a rising golden spiral running through and around the day, bringing all the grace and beauty of Creation into this day, making everything smooth, simple and divine.
6. Connect to the energies that you want to manifest (joy, love, efficiency, structure, communication…) throughout your day and let them be embraced by your heart energy.
7. Then inhale the energies you have, chosen to support you for this task (physical energy, alertness, strength etc).
8. Let the white fire surround you while you send thanks to these supporting energies, to yourself for letting go and your fellow beings, for this day.

Take a deep breath, feel your body balanced and steady on the ground, let out a breathe emerging from your heart, feel the bubbling new energy filling you up, and creating, in your body, the "space-you-need-for-today".

Breathe deeply three times, with the intention to return to the Now, move your arms and legs, open your eyes, smile and just be...

MEDITATE OVER A CUP OF TEA

Intention with this one is to be able to meditate in the quiet presence of others. If you can find peace within, wherever you are, then you can manage stressful situations more easily. Let the moment decide the time dedicated to your moment of silence. If you are at a cafe, use your intuition to find the best spot for you to practice.

- ∂ Light some candles or a table lamp with soft light
- ∂ Turn off the electric light
- ∂ Disconnect your phones
- ∂ Turn of other 'buzzing' electrical devices
- ∂ Find your place where you sit comfortably and in peace
- ∂ Drink your tea with a simple consciousness
- ∂ Let your thoughts come and go in stillness
- ∂ Take small sips
- ∂ Feel the taste
- ∂ Feel how the warmth fills your body
- ∂ Feel your body and sink into the presence of it
- ∂ Think of your breath
- ∂ Use calm breathing to release stress, unwanted thoughts, or what you need in that moment
- ∂ End your tea moment by writing in your diary, picking up your favourite book, listening to some music or going to sleep

SPIRAL MEDITATION

The intention is to create that spiral feel within.
A lot of things are created in spiral form, our DNA, galaxies, and many things in nature start out in spiral form. There are dancing meditations that work in spirals, you can walk in spirals as a way to cleanse and revitalize yourself.

1. Breathe, find your comfort, focus your intention on clearing all your chakras, and send any debris into the White transformative fire. When you feel that you are balanced, breathe out from the center of your heart and start to…
2. Visualize a Blue spiral that embraces you, feel it, be it, merge with it to the core of your hearts being. *Take a breath*
3. Let a Rainbow colored spiral embrace you, feel it, be it, merge with it to the core of your hearts being. *Take a breath*
4. Let a white shimmering spiral embrace you, feel it, be it, merge with it to the core of your hearts being. *Take a breath*
5. Let a golden spiral embrace you, feel it, be it, merge with it to the core of your hearts being.
6. Take a breath and stay in this vibrant energy until you feel that all of your bodies are in total balance. Open your eyes and notice the difference within and without you

EARTH LIGHT MEETS SKY LIGHT

One day I felt this strong energy making its way up through my left foot and at the same time energy came from above making its way down through my right leg. At the same time I had light expanding and moving on my sides of the body. I was curious where all this light was heading, had I just become a vessel of transportation? It ended with me feeling such a balance and peace within. It seems that even if there is a core way to how the energy moves, it is a very individual experience that will give you what you are seeking in that moment. I had to ask my source if I could share this experience and this is what came to me.

1. Be in comfort. It can be an idea to stand up if you really want to feel the energy travel up and down within. Be in the core of your heart and ask the energy transmission to start the dance with you.
2. Breathe with intention to aid the energy to move up and down through you.
3. When the same amount of light is coming from above as well as below (it takes care of this by itself), the light will start to expand towards your sides (left and right).
4. When there is balance on all these levels, the energy is brought into the core of your heart and the light will expand out in front and back of your body
5. You are now one whole being pulsating with Earth and Sky light in all directions.

Let yourself be present in this light and let it take you upon an unexpected, joyful ride.…

THE ANGEL MEDITATION (AROUND A CORNER)

Once when I had a difficulty in accepting what was shown to me in around the corner, I was presented this solution to move forward. I asked that what I perceived, to melt itself down into a sparkling, delicious drink and then I drank it. And by that, I digested the answer too my question and trusted that when it's in, it's going to be cared for my my body / mind and the result would be shown to me, whenever all was done. I usually set a timeframe for how long it shall be processed within and then do the meditation again, to check up on the result.

It has always worked …

There is also a method that you shrink down what you are being shown, into a size that fits your palm and will thereby be easier to view and work with …
If you feel that you are stuck, it can be a special situation. It can be that you cannot understand what you are supposed to understand, to be able to move forward on your path. Looking around "a corner" might help.

1. Be in comfort. Breathe and focus your intention on merging your inner heart and your base chakra so they are in balance. When they dance the same dance, you let this joint energy travel up and embrace your crown and when everything feels in balance you start…
2. Visualize that you are standing in front of a street corner.
3. When you walk around the corner you will perceive "see" what it is you cannot seem to reach to move forward in the situation you need support with.
4. Stand in the power of what you are being shown until it feels that you have accepted the answer.
5. When you feel you are done, breathe and bring yourself back into the core of your heart, move a little and open your eyes.

Sometimes I think it's good to make a little re-cap. To check upon all my inner me's, my inner child, both girl and boy, my teenagers, my inner woman and man, and sometimes even my future woman and man. Life and the transformations that occur are fast and strong, it is possible that a little fragment will be kept lingering somewhere in your bodies.

1. Place yourself in comfort. Breathe from the core of your inner heart and let the light from your heart bring forth a strong feeling of trust and playfulness.

2. Ask your body to create a shimmering rainbow that embraces and cleanses all your chakras. One at the time, start with your crown;

∂ The color of red will enter, and then visualize the rest of the rainbow colors moving through you. When in need, you will most probably feel that all colors are working through you at the same time…

∂ After you have balanced your chakras with the rainbow, the shimmer of your inner core is embracing and surrounding the present You, reaching out to meet your inner You.

3. Inner girl, ask how she is, perceive the answer with the whole of your body and just make a note within you. How old is she? Ask if there is anything she needs from you?

∂ When all is said and created between you, let the girl be immersed in her own light / colour. See her light being embraced by your shimmering light and all becoming One…

4. Then continue to meet and embrace your inner boy, woman, man, etc…

5. When you feel that all is balanced and you have reached an understanding about your "inner family" breathe and bring yourself back into your body, the core of your heart, move your body a little and finally open your eyes. Embrace yourself with a feeling of bravery. You have just brought yourself willingly into the centre of your core and healed yourself on deep, deep levels.

YOUR INNER WOMAN AND MAN MERGING

Intention with this meditation is to clear and balance up old thought forms between your inner man and woman, your active and passive sides.

When it comes to my own thoughts about this, they have varied over the years. I know that I am very balanced between my two sides (I have taken tests) however many people would think that I hold more male energies since I hold a very active personality. I also think that some of us are "a man trapped inside a woman's brain half" and then the result would be a more passive man, and vice versa… so I believe as usual that one should make one's own conclusion and maybe just rest in the fact that we hold a passive and an active side of us, whatever gender, does it really matter?

Within ourselves we both hold a female and a male side. Most commonly we say that the left side holds our female energy and the right side holds the male energy. Keeping these sides in a mutual understanding and balance with each other might take a little work, we usually hold on to thought forms, behaviours, cultural differences not necessarily created by us, they might well be inherited from your family, friends, school etc. To look upon yourself and what you carry, to release this and move on takes courage and trust.

In general we say that the female side holds thoughts, feelings, caring, responsibility and striving for wholeness, more passive. The male side holds freedom, action, justice, more acting out. We tend to place female blockages on our left side and male on our right side. In the society today it is also common that women have to develop more the male side to compete on the same terms as the men. Men on the other hand may have to change how they are if they choose careers that have been more dominated by women over time... like nursing.

This is an example; you want to build a greenhouse in the garden. Your female side plans, writes down everything that is needed and hands it over to the male side that takes the car and buys it all and builds it, then the female side comes and plants it all...

It can be a good idea to write down what you perceive, if you want to do the exercise another time and see what the difference might be …

The meditation is about balancing the two sides within us and this has shown itself to be a powerful way to do that.

1. Sit or lay down in comfort. Breathe and find your pace, imagine a light arising from the core of your heart merging with your brain and then your pelvis (crown & base chakra).
2. Choose the most positive and negative images you have regarding the characters and powers women and men hold. Both within themselves and out to the world.
3. Tune into the brain halves and ask your brain to give you a picture or sense of how each side looks upon itself.
∂ Let the images just flow, don't stop them even if they make no sense, they will in the end, if they seem to never stop, tell your body / brain to sum it up and deliver 6 pictures maximum.
4. Imagine that the pictures you have gathered that belong to your female side, transport themselves over to the male side of your brain and vice versa.
∂ You can choose to do them both at the same time or take one side at the time… if you are very "mental" as in that you believe that your power resides in your mind, try to do both sides at the same side ….
5. After the mix is done, focus on one side and sense it. Can you see, feel, and perceive any difference from the picture or sense you observed before?
6. We people always like to be appreciated for our achievements. The time has come for you to hand over a gift to each side, as a token for a work well done (and to smooth

your ego). Take a breath and tune in with your heart as the main source, to what gift you would like to give each side. When the gifts are clear, go ahead and deliver them to your Inner woman and your Inner man.

7. Take a moment to be and reflect on the feeling of receiving these gifts of love to yourself. Will these change any perspective you hold? Will they hold you in more balance?
   When you are ready, keep an intentional breath of balance, and slowly bring yourself back to the present moment. Move your body a little, open your eyes, and before you start to do anything else, write down how you feel and what you experienced.

PARALLEL LIVES

Intention with this meditation is to find a balance with your daily life and the lives you have perceived from other lifetimes
Keep an open spacious mind and try to just receive what you will perceive during the meditation. Be in the moment of your own truth. Remember to interpret what you perceive as symbols, think about what they mean for you, despite what your friends, books etc will say. It is your mind, your memories, your interpretation...

1. Breathe. Find your comfort, place your intention on your third eye and see the energy merge with the core of your heart. Keep on breathing until you feel that you are balanced in all your bodies and your heart and third eye have a thread of golden shimmer in between them. With some more breaths let the energy of these two surround all of your bodies.
2. Walk into a house of your preference and walk towards an elevator door, light the two candelabras that are placed outside the door and take a look around. How does it look around where you stand?
3. On the table beside the elevator you will find a parcel that you packed for this occasion.
∂ Before you open the door, what feeling do you carry with you?
4. Step into the elevator and press the Go-button. By looking at the panel you can follow where the elevator takes you...
∂ What emotions, thoughts are going through you?
5. When the elevator stops, and the door opens, you are finding yourself standing outside the walls of a city. Find your way to the entrance, go through the gates and stop!
∂ Take a look around. You are looking for a face and when you find it, walk towards each other.

∂ What are you feeling?

6. You and the person whose face you recognised are now standing opposite each other. What feelings pass through you?

∂ Ask for her or his name.

∂ What year is it?

∂ What country are you in?

7. You will now give the person the parcel you brought with you and receive a parcel. What have you packed, what are you being given?

8. When you are ready, you are accompanied back to the place you arrived. You will step back into the elevator and press return.

9. You are back where you started. Blow out the candles and walk out of the house.

10. Slowly by using your breath, breathe back the golden shimmering light you have been surrounded with. When it is back in the core of your heart, slowly move your body and open your eyes.

11. Take a moment and write down your impressions of the journey….

THE BALLOON

The intention with this meditation is to release thought patterns and distrust, and to integrate information and knowledge you have received. For example when your head seems too full to hold any more words, this is a good one to do.

1. Take a few long deep breaths until you are in full contact with your body, the breath is flowing and your limbs are relaxed.

2. Imagine that there is a White fire burning opposite you or in a circle which you create around you…

3. Inhale and let the energy that is stored within your heart (life force, Chi, Prana), expand through your entire body and embrace your whole energy field.

4. Connect to the white fire.

5. Inhale the white transforming light coming from the fire into your heart and let the transforming light fill your bodies with the energy. Sit with this until your physical body feels fully relaxed, your breath is smooth and your limbs relaxed but still energized.

6. Imagine that you have an x-amount of balloons fastened at different places around your body. These symbolize all the knowledge you have received during the workshop,

ceremony etc, which is not yet embodied within you. The energy is waiting to be assimilated to ease your mind and relax your body.

7. Imagine that all the balloons comes together to create one big balloon, that places itself over your head and is anchored at the bottom of your heart.

8. Take a few deep breaths while you breathe in the energy from the one balloon and feel it filling up your entire body down to your feet.

9. All the loose energy (the balloons) is now settled within your body and you can trust that everything you have learned and been through during this period of time is stored at the right places inside your body and mind.

10. Imagine that the thread anchored at the bottom of your heart is released, cutting off the big balloon, travelling up your spine, out of the head and into the white fire in the middle of the circle to be transformed and never to return.

11. Take a last deep breath from the core of your being. Let your body enjoy the space created within and feel how it fills you up and still leaving room for more…

∂ Take a breath. Feel your feet balanced and steady on the ground.

∂ Let a breath emerge from your heart, filled with this new bubbly energy, let the intention of this energy be that it will create a bubble around you, with the exact density, colour, feel you need to be able to hold on and stay in this space you are in now, throughout the whole day.

∂ Take three more deep breaths, with the intention to return to the Now. Move your arms and legs, open your eyes, smile and just be...

HEART TEMPLE

Intention is to bring your own wisdom from the paths you are walking and have walked.
It can be a good idea to have your notebook beside you and be ready to write if needed…
Sometimes I have carried heavy energies inside me, that heavy that I don't want to burden another person with these. I was happy when I found that this meditation brought me to my "source" that I trusted full-hearted and I then was able to handle my work my energies to a release.

1. Be in comfort. Breathe in and out shimmering light that arises from the core of your heart. Bring the shimmer around your whole body and immerse yourself with this light. You are standing on a path, surrounded by light.

2. Start moving forward on the path. Note how it feels walking upon it and how the surroundings are being perceived by your body. Soon you come upon a crossroads. Stay and feel the different energies in all the alternatives you have in front of you.

3. When you have chosen your pathway, note how your body is feeling and keep on walking.

4. Again you are standing in front of a crossroads, feel the different energies in all the alternatives you have in front of you. Start moving and gradually the path you choose will move upwards, you are leaving the ground and are moving upon a more "cosmic" road.

5. You will come upon 3 more crossroads, feel and choose and keep on walking....

6. Finally the road you choose ends on a platform where you are being shown all pathways you have walked upon. You are being shown that some are crossing each other, that they are different in length, that they are broad, narrow, straight, curved but they all are joined in a large weave that leads to the platform...

7. Gazing a little more at the surroundings you notice that the platform is surrounded by the most incredible temples. Choose a temple and walk to it using the cosmic pathways. When you reach the temple feel free to do what you want, rest, dance, explore in the wonderful energy that surrounds this temple.

∂ When you feel ready, please explore other temples, they all carry a special quality.

8. Finally your body will lead you towards the temple of your Inner heart.

∂ This temple has a courtyard where the light emerges very bright and clear, like a White fire. Here you are free to release all that no longer serves you. Choices, beliefs, yours and others, things you have wanted to be free from but you had no sacred place to release into...

∂ Dance within the fire and thank yourself and everyone that have been contributing to the learning you have been through in your life (s), let it all transform and feel how spacious and free your body and mind feels.

9. From the courtyard there is a walkway that leads to a room beaming with the rays of crystals. You will find a crystal day bed where you will lay down and just let yourself be filled with the exact crystal ray you need. Every part of your being will be filled with the exact density and frequency of the crystal it needs. Being filled with all these rays makes you more open towards receiving channelled knowledge from your innermost and Highest self.

10. Open your eyes, get your notebook and pen ready. Write down exactly what comes to you, if its pictures, draw them or describe them and the emotion that opens up within you. Let it flow, let your pen dance and feel free...

11. When you are done in the temple, writing or not, start walking back to the platform, upon a path that will clearly show itself for you, this path will lead you

12. back to Earth, into the room you are in, back into your body, your heart.
13. Slowly breathe yourself back, move a little, gently open your eyes and feel fully returned.

RAINBOW BEACH MEDITATION

The intention of the mediation is to add vibrant colours into the body that might feel a little dull, to create a sense of more balance and fulfilment. The rainbow carries all our chakra colours within. These colours are connected to the physical body. There are also more shimmering colours, pastel colours that belong to your auric field, the more etheric parts of you. Doing a rainbow meditation makes the bodies happy.

1. See yourself walking, the weather is a little cloudy, there is rain hanging above you while you are walking to your favourite beach. There is one spot there, where you know that you can be in total peace, where it is just you and the ocean…
∂ Be aware of the surroundings when you walk, is there anything special that catches your attention?
∂ You have found your place and to honour the day the sun comes shining through the rain clouds and this amazing clear rainbow shows up. It reaches from one end of the beach to the other just where you sit.
2. Let yourself be rinsed by all the colours of the rainbow, let the colours release, merge and uplift your whole body.
∂ Breathe and just be in this moment of tranquillity.
1. After this moment of stillness with the rainbow, you look to the other end of the beach, you feel an urge to walk over to that end and sit down as well.
2. When you reach the other side of the beach, the colours have changed, they are now shimmering pastel colours and you feel that you want to fill your outer bodies, your auric field with them, to be in a complete state of bliss.
3. When you are filled and in balance, just be in your new body and feel how you dance over the beach, that everything you look upon seems to have changed into a more deeper, vibrant energy.

If you like to play with the rainbow, visualize that you are diving down in a lake that has all the colours of the rainbow and swim around and bring the colours within you, when there are no colours left in the water, and you have them inside you, you can come back into this reality.

YOUR DIVINE IMAGE

In our universe you will find a perfect blueprint of yourself. Intention of this meditation is a merger between you in modern time and you in your Divine presence.

See it as the Divine model of your body and the part of your soul that is connected to your bodily dance with the universe. This Divine model is always complete, perfect, dancing in heavenly harmony and balance on all levels, carrying its highest vibration. Many people have a name for this Divine part of themselves or see this as their Higher self. Sometimes it is a nice feeling to re-connect with this Divine blueprint, especially if one has undergone a huge shift in life and feels a little vulnerable. Know what your intentions are. What do you feel that you need to be filled with to be in balance? Or do you trust your Divine You to give you exactly what you need?

1. Breathe. Place yourself in a comfortable position lying on your back. Focus your breath on the inner core of your heart and let the energy merge throughout all of your bodies. When you feel that you are in balance direct your heart energy to connect to your Divine You and her / his heart centre.

2. When you feel that you are in contact, feel how the Divine part of you starts merging with you, a specific shimmer flowing into you, starting from the core of your heart and spreading out into all of your bodies. You are being filled with the highest vibration of freshness, strength into your immune system, balance, and anything else you may need.

3. Continue as long as you want, and when you feel that you are done, start with a focused breath to bring yourself back to your physical body, here and Now.

∂   Make sure that you breathe slowly and "see" all the layers of yourself being brought back through all of your bodies. End with seeing and feeling the shimmering light in the core of your heart.

∂   Gently move your body slowly, stretch out your limbs and finally take some long deep breaths and open your eyes.

THANK YOU FOR READING MY BOOK!

An early Monday in February 2013 when I was clearing my computer, I realized I had the material I needed for the book I had had in the back of my mind for years. A book that gave me the opportunity to work in my home, to develop my skills and find new ways of doing things. A book that somehow gave me the confidence to continue exploring the world of energy.

I love energy! I love the array of possibilities it gives me in how my body and mind has a common language that goes beyond any "reasonable" thoughts and science. The fact that it works makes me happy. I can fly high and low and I can incorporate it with my daily life – today it is my life!

From 2013, up until now, a lot has happened.

The truth is that nothing would have happened in the making of this, if it weren't for my friends, reading and generously sharing opinions. Special thank to the woman who turned it into a book, Nelressa Stalling – I owe her everything, what a sweet and talented soul, the universe brought me.

Anna-Matilda Dahrén, my sister who draw the pictures.

I have had some authors that has inspired me with their knowledge; Ted Andrews, Caroline Myss, Theres Bertherat, Dr Stephen T Chang

When it comes to teachers, my first Reiki teacher Lena Frilund, was all I needed. I started out as her student, moving to assistant, renting space in her studio, and finally she asked if I wanted to manage the healing course she had developed. The level of support she gave me is something I keep close to heart and mind when working with my students. She was my star. Alongside Lena, I have my invisible teachers. My guides and my "aunties" (I travel with many bloodlines this time around) keep me on my toes and make me alert while softly pushing me forward on my life journey. I've had a great source of inspiration and know how in my students and people I have met during workshops I have held or attended. I give great and humble thanks to everyone that made me grow and develop.

If you want to use or reproduce any part of this book, you need a written permission from me.

I am always curious and very interested in learning about your enjoyment whilst reading and working through this book. Please contact me on ewa@mindbodyawakening.com

My wish is that this book will continue to inspire the way I have been inspired.

With LovEwa

Printed in the United States
By Bookmasters